Once a Week

52 small steps on a year-long journey to reach your full potential

David A. Esposito

Independently published through CreateSpace, an Amazon Company.
www.createspace.com

Cover design by Imbue Creative.
www.imbuecreative.com

For additional information and permissions, please contact:
Harvest Time Partners, Inc.
Attention: David Anthony Esposito
Email: david@harvesttimepartners.com

Harvest Time Partners, Inc.
ISBN-13: 978-0692108413 (Custom Universal)
ISBN-10: 0692108416

DEDICATION

This book is dedicated to my children Stephanie, Samantha, David, and Jonathan.

Thanks for the inspiration you have provided me to keep climbing into the ring each and every day.

I hope these small lessons can provide some guidance along your journey to reach your full potential.

I am confident others will say of you, following Homer's comment to a returning warrior, that you are far better than your father and you make glad the heart of your mother.

CONTENTS

DAVID A. ESPOSITO

ACKNOWLEDGMENTS

I want to thank my wife Tracy who has endured an alarm clock at 3:00 AM every Thursday morning for over 5 years as I woke up early to write the **_Character Creates Opportunity_**® blog before the 7:00 AM deadline. Your patience and understanding have been immeasurable.

I want to thank Michael Piperno and the team at Imbue Creative (www.imbuecreative.com). Your support, ideas, and encouragement have given me the courage to take a few leaps into the unknown.

INTRODUCTION

For many of us, life is moving at what seems like light-speed. Work responsibilities demand more time as challenges in the marketplace continue to grow, kids' schedules are jam packed, and then there are the events in the community that require us to do our part to give back. All this activity results in a heightened level of stress and anxiety in the home.

We are all running after a number of very admirable and honorable pursuits. Who can disagree with hard work, preparing kids for a bright future, building a solid career, and doing our part to make the world a better place?

The challenge for all of us is how do we ensure we keep moving in an effective direction to reach our goals while we keep our heads down doing the necessary things today? How do we course correct when our lives come off the rails? How do we find time to reflect on where we have been and where we are headed to ensure it is still where we need to go?

In essence, how do we stay active and engaged on the field of play while we get a view from the coach's box overlooking the field to ensure we are playing at our very best.

The idea for *Once a Week* came out of trying to answer these questions.

It originated with my weekly blog called ***Character Creates Opportunity***®. New content has been available every Thursday morning for over five years. The blog's intent is to support and encourage readers to reach their full potential through the building and strengthening of their character. At

1

Harvest Time Partners — a company that my wife Tracy and I founded more than 20 years ago to provide resources that help individuals and families reach their full potential in an increasingly complex and uncertain world — we believe that Character Creates Opportunity to reach our hopes and dreams, regardless of our situation.

The content for **Once a Week** came from Harvest Time Partners' most popular blog posts over the years. Each weekly reading concludes with some thought-provoking questions to help ensure readers remain on an effective path to reach their full potential.

It is my hope that readers will commit a relatively small amount of time, approximately 30 minutes, **Once a Week**, to reinforce what is important in their lives and get re-energized to climb back into the ring for another week to reach their full potential in their most important roles in the home, the workplace, and the community.

As you begin this once a week journey, here are a few introductory comments to help build a foundation for the journey.

Why is character so important?

In order to answer that question, it is important to address some universal truths in our world.

1. We will experience both ups and downs, great highs and great lows. Whether it is in school, work, our community, and certainly in our homes, we will encounter situations that provide us with opportunities to grow.

2. There are always three elements to every one of our experiences:

    a **SITUATION**: There is our present situation. Many times, our situation is beyond our immediate, personal control, like the weather, an emergency customer call late at night, a reckless driver, an outburst from an individual in an overwhelming situation, etc.

    a **GAP**: There is a gap, a moment in our consciousness where we form our response to the situation. The gap could be a split second or a longer period of time.

    a **RESPONSE**: There is our response to the situation.

3. How we fill the GAP will determine our potential and emotional health. In the GAP, lies our character. We are not confined to a stimulus-response type paradigm like we see in wild animals. Our unique human qualities provide us with the freedom to choose our response to our situation. We possess the potential to rise above our situation by effectively using the GAP between our SITUATION and our RESPONSE.

Our character is *Standing in the Gap*® between our situation and our response.

Our character is our inner voice (our internal compass) that guides our thoughts, decisions, and actions. When we guide our thoughts, decisions, and actions by principles like courage, loyalty, honesty, teamwork, and commitment, we build and strengthen our character. As our character is strengthened, we widen the GAP to develop our most effective response. Our most effective response to our present situation will eventually lead to improved situations in the future, which will form the foundation to achieve even greater goals and places us on an effective path to reach our full potential.

It is in the gap between a situation and our response where we have the opportunity to reach our full potential. Our character is **Standing in the Gap** and that is why character is the critical catalyst to reaching our full potential.

One important reminder is that as we face situations in life, there is **ALWAYS** a gap between that situation and our response. How we fill that gap will determine our potential and emotional health.

I hope this *Once a Week* journey will feed and nourish you in a most helpful and relevant way.

Please feel free to reach out to me if I can help you in your journey. I wish you all the best.

Be well my friend.

David
david@harvesttimepartners.com

PS: One final note; The readers of this book will most likely be adults. However, I would like to reinforce that the development of character begins early in life.

"Good habits formed in youth make all the difference."

Aristotle

"You know that the beginning is the most important part of any work, especially in the case of a young and tender thing; for that is the time at which the character is being formed and the desired impression is more readily taken...Anything received into the mind at that age is likely to become indelible and unalterable; and therefore it is most important that the tales which the young first hear should be models of virtuous thoughts..."

Plato's Republic

For those readers who have a connection to children, please consider that the teachings in **Once a Week** can help children start and stay on an effective path to reach their full potential.

ONCE A WEEK

DAVID A. ESPOSITO

1

BUILDING MOMENTUM

The positive financial impact of compounding interest is well known and has been reinforced by some of the brightest minds in our history. Benjamin Franklin described compounding as "Money can beget money, and its offspring can beget more." A quote commonly attributable to Albert Einstein is, "Compounding is mankind's greatest invention because it allows for the reliable, systematic accumulation of wealth." Compound interest is one way our money can make more money. It is a simple, yet effective way of gaining momentum in the journey to build financial strength.

As we continue on our journey to build and strengthen our character, the concept of compounding interest can provide some insight into building momentum to reach our hopes and dreams. Before we go there, it is important to first acknowledge that we all have an element of our nature that wants a quick fix to our struggles or a fast track to achieving our life-long goals. We want financial security now, and there is a strong appeal to some quick, potentially high-return investment. We listen to a motivational speaker at some high-energy conference and we expect great results on day one. We attend a weekend marriage retreat and plan to apply the "5 principles of a great marriage" on Monday and then we expect to finally have the relationship we desire. We get the DVD series and new juice blender to lose 20 pounds in 2 weeks and we believe we have found the fountain of youth (we have cabinets full of these DVDs and blenders in case any of you are wondering).

The reality is that quick, lasting fixes don't happen in the major and most important areas of our life. As we think about the principle of compounding interest, there are some relevant learnings that compounding can have in

7

many areas of our lives beyond finance. When we look at a graph of building financial strength with compounding over time, the 'wealth curve' appears relatively flat in the early years and then slowly builds momentum and the curve gets very steep in later years. The consistent application of some small dollar amount placed in a savings or investment portfolio will put any one of us on the path to building a small fortune over time. The principle is that we need to stick with it, leave the money alone, and let the interest grow.

Guiding our thoughts, decisions, and actions by the principle of compounding in other areas of our lives can help build momentum to reach our goals.

In Relationships:

There are probably many things we can do to improve the relationships of those closest to us. There are countless books and blogs out there to help all of us. Applying the principle of compounding by making a decision to do something small and consistent over time will help. For example, we could just focus on being a better listener. When we feel like immediately jumping in with a comment or correction, if, just once a day, we held back and focused on listening with the intent to understand the other person, we would be on a better path to building strong relationships with those who matter most. Just changing our behavior once a day in conversations will build momentum in our relationships and the compounding interest curve will continue to rise with the eventual outcome being healthier relationships.

In Health and Wellness:

We all have struggles with some aspect of staying physically healthy. For some it is overeating, others it is getting little to no exercise, for still others a lack of sleep can contribute to health problems. There are plenty of resources out there to help us get on the right path to improving our health. With the principle of compounding, find one small, relevant step we can do and stick with it. Perhaps leaving a few bites of dessert behind is a potential step to take or drinking one less can of soda throughout the day. For others it may be walking one more lap around the block or maybe 5 more minutes of some cardio-workout. The point is that whatever the choice, making one small change, consistently over time, will pay tremendous interest over time with regards to our health and wellness. There is a great deal of academic research and practical experience to dispute the lasting impact of any extreme fad diet or exercise regimen. However, the consistent application of small incrementally positive steps toward improving our health will make a lasting impact.

In Personal Development:

We all have areas we need to improve professionally and personally. Perhaps attending some high-energy seminar will kick us into gear to take the first step. However, it will be small incremental changes that will bring about lasting change. For example, reading books relevant to our chosen profession for 15 minutes a day or keeping a daily journal of progress toward some goal are small steps, that over time, have proven to produce huge dividends in personal growth and accomplishment. These actions start small, build over time, and gain momentum to have a positive sustainable impact.

Remember the compounding of interest…just keep making steady, small, consistent steps in the right direction and the results will be tremendous over the long haul. The curve will be relatively flat at first, but it will get steeper over time. It is how we finish, not the "dash and flash" at the start, that really matters. As we continue to apply the principle of compounding in other areas of our life, we will continue to build and strengthen our character, and our *Character Creates Opportunity* for us to make a real difference in our world.

Questions to Dig Deeper

Have I accepted the truth that there are no quick fixes to the important things in life?

What small step can I take to ensure I commit to positive change in an important area of my life?

Weekly Reflections

What have I learned and/or how have I grown in the prior week?

_____

_____

What are my hopes for the week ahead?

_____

_____

What three things am I thankful for that could be a source of encouragement to me in the week ahead?

(1) _____

(2) _____

(3) _____

How am I serving and sacrificing in the important areas of my life?

Family and Friends: _____

_____

Work: _____

_____

Community: _____

_____

What small steps can I take this week to continue to build and strengthen my character?

In my thoughts:

_____

In my decisions:

_____

In my actions:

_____

2

THE IMPORTANCE OF LISTENING

There seems to be no shortage of talkers in our world. Traditional media, our school systems, and our workplaces are all wired to recognize and reward the talkers.

As we continue on our journey to build and strengthen our character in a world that highlights the loud and proud, we don't want to miss the power of listening to build healthy relationships, open dialogue with those who are hurting, and establish the foundation to reach our hopes and dreams.

We all cherish the moment when we are truly being listened to and understood.

There are plenty of "experts" who would describe the importance of listening to others as a key ingredient to understand another person; and through understanding, we can begin to build better relationships. In addition, I am sure we have all experienced the occasional "aha" moment when we finally shut-up long enough to listen and gained some real insight into understanding another person and why they have a certain point of view or why they took a certain action.

Just recently, some exciting new research has been released that demonstrates the power of our brains to relate to one another when we truly listen. Research out of Princeton being led by neuroscientist Uri Hasson went beyond traditional techniques of simply mapping activity in particular regions of the brain. Dr. Hasson's research used complex mathematical analyses to map patterns of activity in the brain. The research added the dimension of measuring the relationship between the pattern in one person's brain and the pattern in another's.

The research team recorded the brain activity of one person's brain while they told a story and another person's brain who was listening. The two brain patterns showed a remarkable degree of correlation. The storyteller had literally gotten into the listener's brain and altered it not only on the logic-reasoning parts of the brain, but most importantly, on the emotional part. By focusing on listening, the listener was able to match the brain of the storyteller. The listener felt the emotions of the storyteller.

The research demonstrated over and over that when you listen to and understand another person, you experience the exact same brain pattern as that person. It is as if you have experienced their experience. The research demonstrated that our brains know little difference between our own experience and one we shared by listening to another. Our brains are impacted the same way. Listening to another person can provide real insight into another person's journey and help us understand.

In addition to these types of research insights and the so-called "experts" in the field, here are just a few thoughts to reinforce the importance of listening to build healthy relationships:

1. Listening is the most simple and powerful way to demonstrate to someone that they matter. Our decision to listen meets a very important psychological need in all of us — to know we matter. Listening does not take a PhD in psychology, an extremely high IQ, or some position in the corner office. All it takes is a simple decision to be silent and give someone our attention.

2. As our world continues to grow more intense and complex, before we instinctively move to shout out our "brilliant opinion," we should first choose to listen. As the research showed, when we listen, we actually feel the experience of the other person. This is a relevant and practical choice for our home, our workplace, and our community. As with many other things, the greatest challenge is often listening to those who are closest to us in our home. We mistakenly think we know them well enough because we have lived with them for so long that we don't need to listen. In addition, we may have allowed the obstacles of anger, frustration, and apathy to prevent us from listening to the other side of the story…and there is always another side to the story.

3. For most people, it is our painful experiences that have taught us the most and form the basis for many of the choices we make. However, we typically keep hidden those painful experiences from others. Being a good listener can help build a trusting, non-judgmental, and shame-free atmosphere, which can eventually open a door to the sharing of those painful experiences to assist in a greater understanding of one another. Understanding is the foundation for health in our relationships.

Listening, with the intent to understand, is a well-documented and practical approach to improve relationships. As we make the decision to listen, we will build and strengthen our character, and **Character Creates Opportunity** to build healthy and meaningful relationships.

Questions to Dig Deeper

Who are the people I care about most who would benefit if I improved my ability and commitment to listen better?

What small step can I take to be a better listener to those I care about most?

Weekly Reflections

What have I learned and/or how have I grown in the prior week?

_____

_____

What are my hopes for the week ahead?

_____

_____

What three things am I thankful for that could be a source of encouragement to me in the week ahead?

(1) _____

(2) _____

(3) _____

How am I serving and sacrificing in the important areas of my life?

Family and Friends: _____

_____

Work: _____

_____

Community: _____

_____

What small steps can I take this week to continue to build and strengthen my character?

In my thoughts:

_____

In my decisions:

_____

In my actions:

_____

3

GENTLENESS

As we continue on our journey to build and strengthen our character, today's theme is about a principle that gets little mention in today's "loud and proud" environment. When we call roll for those who have delivered lasting, positive impact in our world, in our communities, and most certainly in our homes, there is a common virtue among them that is tough to find in the intensity of our world today.

The quality of gentleness — or "strength under control" as the more practical, relevant definition — continues to be an effective behavioral anchor in dealing with relationships in the complexity of life today.

I am confident that if I polled the readers of this book, we could all give a few solid testimonies about when we "lost it" in a relatively intense or even seemingly routine interaction with a family member, coworker, or friend. We occasionally blame our response on the hectic commute across town, a stressful day at work, the loss of the big game, our finances, the weather, etc. However, we all know we fell short in demonstrating strength under control. We most likely took a big withdrawal out of the proverbial "relationship bank account" and needed to work extra hard making deposits into the future if we wanted to repair the relationship.

Maintaining gentleness in today's world is not easy. The real-life situations of dealing with an unruly child while hustling to get ready for work, an irate customer call just as "normal business hours" have passed and your daycare is closing, the spouse who just seems oblivious to the situation you are struggling to get through, or the aging parent who does not realize her limitations are all situations that put our gentleness to the test. It is not easy to maintain strength under control, but it is well worth the effort.

There are several positive outcomes that we can all expect by demonstrating a greater degree of gentleness or strength under control in our interactions with others:

1. Gentleness has been shown over time, either through time-tested philosophers or academic research, to be the more effective method in strengthening relationships and sustaining positive behavioral change compared to the typical "loud, proud, and loss of control" technique we all so quickly adopt.

2. We will quickly replace the regretful thought of "oh, I should not have acted that way" with the cherished memory that we did the harder right, rather than the easier wrong, and more times than not, maintained a productive connection to continue the relationship another day.

3. Our example will be "watched" by those around us, and whether we ever see it or not, others will be positively impacted by our actions.

One final note of truth from the late Leo Buscaglia, PhD. I am not sure if you remember Leo, but he was "Dr. Love" in the 70s and 80s who was famous for his sold-out "Love 1A" class at the University of Southern California. His PBS Specials (which are on YouTube for those interested) were an earlier and less rehearsed version of modern day TED Talks for healthy relationships. Leo Buscaglia, in describing a relevant truth of those exhibiting the virtue of gentleness said, "Only the weak are cruel. Gentleness can only be expected from the strong."

We should all strive to be strong and model the principle of gentleness. As a result, we will continue to make steady progress on building and strengthening our character, and ***Character Creates Opportunity*** for us to have a positive, lasting impact in our relationships.

Questions to Dig Deeper

When were some times in the past when I did not act in a gentle way toward those I care about most?

What small step can I take to demonstrate gentleness toward those I care about most?

<u>Weekly Reflections</u>

What have I learned and/or how have I grown in the prior week?

_____

_____

What are my hopes for the week ahead?

_____

_____

What three things am I thankful for that could be a source of encouragement to me in the week ahead?

(1) _____

(2) _____

(3) _____

How am I serving and sacrificing in the important areas of my life?

Family and Friends: _____

_____

Work: _____

_____

Community: _____

_____

What small steps can I take this week to continue to build and strengthen my character?

In my thoughts:

_____

In my decisions:

_____

In my actions:

_____

4

THE BRIGHT SIDE OF LONELINESS

If we chose to believe the statistics, either we or someone close to us on our left or right struggles with feeling alone. If we take an honest reflection of our own lives, there are probably times when we felt the sense of being out there all alone facing a particular situation:

- In the workplace, we can feel alone in dealing with a difficult boss, being a part of a project team that just doesn't function like a team, or when we lost that "critical" account and everyone is turning their eyes on us.
- In school, when the "cool" group leaves us behind or we stayed home instead of attending the big party, we can feel a bit lonely.
- In the home, we can feel alone during times of struggle in a marriage, children whose birth order may align with certain experiences (it is more than just the middle child syndrome), or when adult children start making life choices that conflict with the hopes of parents.

We can all feel lonely from time to time.

There were two times in my adult life when I have walked down the road with a close friend facing a terminal illness. In both experiences, they commented how wonderful it was to have family and friends around to help them in their most difficult situation. However, both of them, from very different backgrounds and walks of life, made the same comment to me that even with all these people around, their journey down that final road is an extremely lonely one.

As we continue to build and strengthen our character, embracing the bright side of loneliness will help each of us reach our full potential throughout the ups and downs of life in our home, the workplace, and community.

Like most things in life, we can view challenges as a reminder of our own weaknesses or we can use challenges as opportunities to learn and grow. We make that choice every day, and dealing with loneliness is no different. We have a choice. There was some recent published research on the best ways of coping with loneliness, and of all the options like group therapy, community intervention, pharmaceutical treatments, etc., the most effective was some individual support to encourage changing our own thoughts and beliefs about ourselves.

As we view these occasions of loneliness as opportunities to grow, here are a few ways to remind us of the bright side of loneliness.

1. **The first step towards self-improvement.** The quiet of loneliness is a helpful place because the first step of any great movement starts with struggles in the present. In the quiet of loneliness, quite often we can see the need for change. Whether it is in our careers to find something purposeful that excites us, or in our educational pursuits to study something that can help us to have a real positive impact, or in our homes to take steps to be a better spouse or parent. Our desire to improve our situation starts with some dissatisfaction of the present. In the cold quiet of loneliness, we often find the spark to ignite positive change in our lives.

2. **We can make a quick turnaround.** In the final assessment, making a shift in mindset is all up to us. There is empowerment and energy that comes with standing and facing our situation alone without the challenges of miscommunication, unmet expectations, or half-hearted commitments that sometimes come with large group efforts. We can move quickly in guiding our own thoughts, decisions, and actions. As we look into the mirror, we need to ask, "What are we waiting for?"

3. **A helping hand to others.** Our journey through loneliness can be a helpful source of encouragement to someone who needs it most. We should be genuine and authentic in sharing our journey with someone else. As Plato once said, "Be kind, for everyone you meet is fighting a harder battle." Someone close to us may need to hear

our example of overcoming, but they may be too ashamed, embarrassed, or hurt to ask. Sharing our journey with those we care about most should be thought of as a potential source of encouragement to them, not a needed badge of honor for ourselves.

As we choose to see the bright side of loneliness, we can increase our chances of overcoming. We will continue to build and strengthen our character, and *Character Creates Opportunity* to reach our full potential and have a positive impact on others.

Questions to Dig Deeper

When were some times when I felt all alone?

When I feel alone, what small step can I take to see the experience as an opportunity to learn and grow?

Weekly Reflections

What have I learned and/or how have I grown in the prior week?

_____

_____

What are my hopes for the week ahead?

_____

_____

What three things am I thankful for that could be a source of encouragement to me in the week ahead?

(1) _____

(2) _____

(3) _____

How am I serving and sacrificing in the important areas of my life?

Family and Friends: _____

_____

Work: _____

_____

Community: _____

_____

What small steps can I take this week to continue to build and strengthen my character?

In my thoughts:

_____

In my decisions:

_____

In my actions:

_____

5

THE LONG VIEW

The bookstore shelves (or Amazon.com) are lined with helpful hints on handling difficult relationships and tips on how to handle conflict with someone important in our lives. These resources help address the reality that we don't live on an island. Life is about relationships and relationships, even with the best intentions, will get complicated, strained, and a bit sloppy from time to time.

The important relationships in our home, workplace, and community are worth our best effort to keep them moving forward in a positive direction. With this book, we have often discussed the importance of understanding one another because of the cold reality that we each see the world as we are, not as it is. Deep understanding of each other's point of view often leads to forgiveness, and forgiveness brings about the opportunity for redemption, even when relationships have become broken and shattered.

As we continue on our journey to build and strengthen our character, an important principle to sustain healthy relationships is taking the long view in our day-to-day interactions with those important in our lives.

If we agree with most relationship experts and perhaps our own honest reflection of our life's journey, we would see that most of us have a tough time with difficult conversations with those closest to us. One of the great dichotomies of life is that conflict of ideas and decisions in the home, workplace, and community can create real difficult situations, but confrontation, healthy discourse, and diversity of opinions are the life blood of organizations and families. *(Take heart parents who argue frequently…research says our kids will be better able to think on their own because they constantly see their parents with different opinions, which drives them to think for themselves because their parents certainly haven't solved it for them. For those of you who have the "perfect" relationship with no disagreements or where that "one person" always gets his/her way, be forewarned, your kids may not be well prepared to handle life's inevitable differences of opinion.)*

If we take the time to reflect back over conflicts and difficult conversations, quite often we realize we made a mountain out of a mole hill, the issue that brought about the conflict was not the "real" issue, or it just was not a really big deal after all. Time is a great counselor because it gives us perspective.

One of the most difficult interpersonal challenges we all face is how to take a long-term perspective in the heat of the moment.

There is always a gap between our situation and how we respond. Standing in that gap is our opportunity to take the long view. Principles such as understanding, responsibility, loyalty, and commitment, help us to rise above the heat of the moment and widen that gap to create a more constructive interaction to solve difficult problems.

When we choose to take the long view in the gap between our situation and our response, we take several steps towards sustaining health in our important relationships:

1. We focus on the principle and not the person. If there was dishonesty in the situation, we focus on the breakdown of an important principle. We don't just call someone a lying, selfish jerk. Addressing the principle without attacking the person opens the door for dialogue.

2. Timeless and universal principles such as honesty, loyalty, and commitment give us a strong foundation to more effectively see others' points of view. Our foundation on principle also helps keep our own emotions in check in the heat of the moment.

3. We set an example for others to follow…our character stands in the gap between our situation and our response, and principle-based behavior is contagious.

We have tremendous potential for growth and development as we stand in the gap between our situation and our response with thoughts, decisions, and actions based on principles such as loyalty, commitment, and perseverance. As we stand on timeless and universal principles, we will continue to build and strengthen our character, and *Character Creates Opportunity* to build healthy relationships that grow stronger rather than weaker with different perspectives and the conflict that results.

Questions to Dig Deeper

When was a time when I made a "mountain out of a mole hill" with someone close to me?

What small step can I take to ensure I pause and take a long-term perspective in my day-to-day dealings with the people I care about most?

Weekly Reflections

What have I learned and/or how have I grown in the prior week?

_____

_____

What are my hopes for the week ahead?

_____

_____

What three things am I thankful for that could be a source of encouragement to me in the week ahead?

(1) _____

(2) _____

(3) _____

How am I serving and sacrificing in the important areas of my life?

Family and Friends: _____

_____

Work: _____

_____

Community: _____

_____

What small steps can I take this week to continue to build and strengthen my character?

In my thoughts:

_____

In my decisions:

_____

In my actions:

_____

6

A MOST NEEDED GIFT

We spend a great deal of time, effort, and money thinking about the perfect gift for friends and family for birthdays and holidays. We are continually bombarded by special deals, discounts, free shipping, and "gotta have it" gift items throughout the year.

As we continue on our journey to build and strengthen our character, there is a principle that is at the heart of one of the most needed gifts we can provide those around us. The principle of encouragement can help to bolster the positive impact we desire to have on others. Encouragement is a most needed gift that we can readily give to those around us.

There has been a great deal of research done on the importance of the principle of encouragement. We can probably all remember a time when someone, a close family member, friend, teacher, coach, or boss shared a word of encouragement when "quit" looked good and we were in a dark valley wondering how things were going to turn out. Encouragement is a most needed gift.

As today's world continues to grow in complexity and uncertainty, the principle of encouragement can go a long way to assist those around us to keep moving forward in pursuit of their hopes and dreams despite the challenges they face.

A word of encouragement provides several benefits to an individual:

1. Encouragement helps to meet an important need in all of us; the need to know we belong. It reminds us that someone is interested in us and our present situation.

2. Encouragement demonstrates that someone believes in our potential. In a world with a natural bent toward the negative, encouragement helps all of us refocus on a positive point of view, which consistently proves to be the differentiator between people achieving goals and those who fall short.

3. Encouragement reminds us that we should have high expectations. Many times, we can let self-doubt and fear steal our potential to do great things. Encouragement helps us fix our eyes on the unlimited potential we have to make a difference in this world.

An important role we can all play is in helping others reach their full potential. As we become more intentional about using the principle of encouragement, we will continue to build and strengthen our character, and *Character Creates Opportunity* to help others more effectively face the inevitable challenges in life and keep them moving forward along the path to reach their hopes and dreams.

Questions to Dig Deeper

When was the last time I encouraged someone close to me?

What small step can I take to be more encouraging to those I care about most?

Weekly Reflections

What have I learned and/or how have I grown in the prior week?

_____

_____

What are my hopes for the week ahead?

_____

_____

What three things am I thankful for that could be a source of encouragement to me in the week ahead?

(1) _____

(2) _____

(3) _____

How am I serving and sacrificing in the important areas of my life?

Family and Friends: _____

_____

Work: _____

_____

Community: _____

_____

What small steps can I take this week to continue to build and strengthen my character?

In my thoughts:

_____

In my decisions:

_____

In my actions:

_____

DAVID A. ESPOSITO

7

THE PERSONAL SIDE OF FREEDOM

We all appreciate freedom.

The freedom to come and go as we please. The freedom to live according to a set of beliefs. The freedom to pursue our hopes and dreams. The list could go on and on.

One person who understood freedom very well was the late Nelson Mandela (1918–2013, former President of South Africa).

On February 11, 1990, Nelson Mandela, after 27 years in prison, walked out of a South African prison into freedom, but he was not totally free. It was not until he made one more decision that truly set him free. "As I walked out the door toward the gate that would lead to my freedom, I knew if I didn't leave my bitterness and hatred behind, I'd still be in prison."

If we all reflected on the following questions, how would we respond?

1. Have we ever been misguided by a friend or family member?

2. Have we ever been treated unfairly in the workplace?

3. Have we ever put our heart and soul into a relationship that subsequently fell apart?

4. Have we ever had someone we trusted take advantage of that trust?

Chances are pretty good that we all would answer "yes" to many, if not all, of the questions above.

Given the affirmative response to many of these questions, an important reality we need to face is the level of bitterness and anger we still hold around those events and those individuals. To use Mandela's concept, are we still in prison because of those feelings?

As we continue to build and strengthen our character, we need to ask ourselves an important question, "If I am holding on to bitterness and anger from the past, am I really free?"

This other side of freedom is different than the 4th of July kind of freedom we experience in America. This other side of freedom is a result of the individual choice we make to leave bitterness behind and move on.

If we let bitterness and anger from the past define our future, we will not reach our full potential.

Here are just a few ideas to help us move towards the personal freedom we need to reach our full potential:

- **We all make mistakes**. We have probably caused some pain to others we wish we had not. Extend the same forgiveness and understanding we wish others would do for us.

- **It will happen again**. Life is complicated, and people react in different ways. We need to be careful that we don't become disillusioned with expectations that life will be clean and nice and our closest relationships will be like the fairy tales we read as a kid. Life is messy and complicated. There will be misunderstandings and pain along the journey.

- **Bitterness and anger hold us back**. Once we learn to forgive and move on, we will experience the benefits of being free from the anger of the past. We will develop the "muscle memory" to forgive quickly, remove negative emotions, and apply ourselves fully to achieve our hopes and dreams.

- **We set an example for others to follow**. The more we can demonstrate the ability to remove bitterness over past events, the more others will see our actions and follow…especially those closest to home whom we hope can have the best foundation to reach their full potential.

As we make the choice to leave behind bitterness and anger from the unfortunate events of our past, we will continue to build and strengthen our character, and **Character Creates Opportunity** to reach our full potential and have a great impact on those around us.

<u>Questions to Dig Deeper</u>

Do I still hold onto bitterness and anger from some past painful events?

What small step can I take to minimize or leave behind those feelings?

<u>Weekly Reflections</u>

What have I learned and/or how have I grown in the prior week?

_____

_____

What are my hopes for the week ahead?

_____

_____

What three things am I thankful for that could be a source of encouragement to me in the week ahead?

(1) _____

(2) _____

(3) _____

How am I serving and sacrificing in the important areas of my life?

Family and Friends: _____

_____

Work: _____

_____

Community: _____

_____

What small steps can I take this week to continue to build and strengthen my character?

In my thoughts:

_____

In my decisions:

_____

In my actions:

_____

8

A PERSISTENT ADVERSARY

We all understand the importance of setting clear goals, both near term and long term, in order to accomplish important objectives in our lives. There is a fairly sizeable body of evidence in both academic circles and practical experience to indicate that we build strength to persevere towards our goals when we can see clearly what we are trying to achieve.

As we continue on our own personal journey to build and strengthen our character, there is a common and persistent adversary that we all face in trying to reach our goals and make meaningful progress toward our own personal vision for our life.

The common and persistent adversary that comes against each one of us at various points in our journey has numerous descriptions, but it can be summarized as fear, anxiety, and worry. This adversary has the potential to drain that precious energy we need to keep moving forward towards our goals and many times, this adversary can be forceful enough to get us off track and switch our long-term view entirely.

We all have various coping mechanisms to deal with fear, anxiety, and worry. Some of us are nail-bitters, some toss and turn through a sleepless night, some repeat simple, routine tasks, some take pills, some overeat, some don't eat, and some drink alcohol a little more often during the rough times in the journey. Regardless of our coping mechanism, the reality is that we still have that persistent adversary attempting to sabotage our efforts to reach our goals.

As we continue on our journey to build and strengthen our character, below are a few ideas to deal effectively with our common, persistent adversary:

- **Acknowledge the reality**. We all face fear, anxiety, and worry. We should possess the courage to call them out directly and not deny their existence. No matter what phase of life we are in and no matter what level of worldly accomplishment or "validation" event we have passed through, we will still face fear, anxiety, and worry as we transition into the next turn in life.

- **Take action**. The best-known antidote to fear, anxiety, and worry is action. When we take small steps toward goals, the adversary loses its grip. Just like the "butterflies" before a big game, after the first play, they are gone, and we are focused on the task at hand. The biggest risk we face in dealing with fear, anxiety, and worry is that we don't get out of bed and get in the game. The simple task of just getting up and facing the challenge is often all we need to do in order to weaken this persistent adversary.

- **Keep the faith**. The very fact that we are still standing is testament to the fact that we have already passed through some difficult challenges in the past. Whether they were in school, in the home, in the workplace, or in some other endeavor, we faced this adversary before and we overcame. Whether we describe our faith in terms of a relationship with God who knows the whole story, or we have faith in the truth found in principles like perseverance and courage, we should rally our faith to keep moving forward against this persistent adversary.

We will continue to face struggles as we journey towards achieving our goals. When we possess the courage to stand up and face fear, worry, and anxiety, we will continue to build and strengthen our character, and ***Character Creates Opportunity*** for us to make meaningful progress towards achieving our goals and motivating those around us to overcome their own challenges.

Questions to Dig Deeper

When have I let fear and worry impact my thoughts and decisions?

What small step can I take to more effectively deal with fear and worry?

Weekly Reflections

What have I learned and/or how have I grown in the prior week?

_____

_____

What are my hopes for the week ahead?

_____

_____

What three things am I thankful for that could be a source of encouragement to me in the week ahead?

(1) _____

(2) _____

(3) _____

How am I serving and sacrificing in the important areas of my life?

Family and Friends: _____

_____

Work: _____

_____

Community: _____

_____

What small steps can I take this week to continue to build and strengthen my character?

In my thoughts:

In my decisions:

In my actions:

9

FAMILY TRANSITION

Many of our struggles with work, finances, career choices, and even health issues have a natural ebb and flow throughout our journey of life. If we gathered up all the academic research in human psychology, talked to countless numbers of "life-coaching" gurus, and reflected back on our own lives, we would all describe that despite our world growing more complex and intense, the most difficult and lasting struggles are still found in the home.

Family conflicts are the most heart-breaking of all of life's toughest problems.

When we separate out the "typical" short-term ups and downs, we come to a clear conclusion that most long-term, sustaining family conflicts have their beginnings during the major transition points in life. Just to state a few of the obvious ones:

- **Transition into marriage.** "Two become one" is a lot easier said than done.

- **Transition into parenting.** Time, effort, commitment, and unconditional love take on a whole new level of understanding.

- **Transition for children to adolescence and to adulthood.** Moving from "being taught" to "choosing to learn" is a responsibility that not everyone wants to accept.

- **Transition of parenting.** The parental struggles of purpose and meaning when grown children become exactly what we want them to be, self-sufficient to take on the world.

- **Transition of generations.** The grandparent struggle for purpose and meaning when grown children and grandchildren are actively engaged in the building of their own lives.

- **Transition of life and death.** The struggle with the loss and the legacy.

Probably the most difficult of all transitions in the home is the mental and emotional transition from expectation (or "fairy tale") to reality. We all grew up with a certain expectation of what family was all about. As adults, we come to realize our reality may not be what we originally planned.

As we continue on our journey to build and strengthen our character, handling the many transitions in life provides abundant opportunities to reinforce the importance of principles like commitment, courage, and loyalty.

Here are a few suggestions to support and encourage a more intentional family engagement to deal with the tension that occurs through life's most critical transitions:

1. **Regroup.** Whether it is a marriage that has fallen off the tracks or families seeing a lack of care and concern, someone needs the courage to be the catalyst to "gather around the table" and raise the issue. Avoidance is not a healthy option. We don't need to wait for a brilliant solution to emerge, we just need the courage to start the discussion.

2. **Understanding.** This time (as we all probably fell short the first go around), genuinely try to understand the other person's point of view. Too often we are continually angling to have our point of view "win." For perhaps the first time ever, focus all effort on trying to understand the other person's point of view to a level that we can describe it back to his/her satisfaction. Then and only then, should we proceed with raising our point of view. It has been my experience, that when I have tried to put this into practice, my supposedly "brilliant" point of view was not even relevant to the real issue at hand. Understanding is the most critical step along the path to resolving family conflict.

3. **Try a different approach.** Albert Einstein once said, "The problems that exist in the world today cannot be solved by the level of thinking that created them." We need to come to the reality that the quick fixes that may have worked in the past are most likely irrelevant today. A new approach, anchored on timeless principles like honesty, loyalty, and commitment, should be our rallying cry.

If the three points above don't work for you and when all else fails, just take the advice of one of my children who has a discerning heart to sense conflict in our home and simply have the courage to say, "I need a hug." Believe it or not, there is an overwhelming amount of research to show that a physical touch can break down walls of conflict in the home. Even when tensions are high, both sides in the home should find the courage to touch. It has been shown to make all the difference in getting on the right path to healing the wounds suffered during a family conflict.

As we develop the courage to regroup and seek understanding and a different approach, we will build and strengthen our character, and *Character Creates Opportunity* to effectively address the most difficult of all of life's struggles, family conflicts.

Questions to Dig Deeper

What are some difficult family conflicts that I continue to experience?

What small steps can I take to more effectively deal with these conflicts?

Weekly Reflections

What have I learned and/or how have I grown in the prior week?

_____

_____

What are my hopes for the week ahead?

_____

_____

What three things am I thankful for that could be a source of encouragement to me in the week ahead?

(1) _____

(2) _____

(3) _____

How am I serving and sacrificing in the important areas of my life?

Family and Friends: _____

_____

Work: _____

_____

Community: _____

_____

What small steps can I take this week to continue to build and strengthen my character?

In my thoughts:

_____

In my decisions:

_____

In my actions:

_____

10

THE OTHER SIDE OF SUFFERING

There is a great deal written, discussed, and testimonies given about the various disappoints, discomforts, and sufferings we endure during our journey of life.

Some of these are relatively light-hearted sufferings like a missed plane, a canceled meeting, the consistently late cable guy, or the important phone call that was dropped while navigating a big-city traffic jam.

However, many of us would classify some sufferings as almost too much to endure, like the untimely death of a loved one, a parent holding the hand of a terminally ill child, the heartbreaking destruction of a once close family, or the addiction that resulted in a tragic ending.

Although we all hope to avoid a great deal of pain and suffering in this world, the reality is that we all will endure our share of suffering. Most of us will find a way to carry on, some in silence and some with a loud roar. There is no escaping disappointment, discouragement, and suffering. Our typical pathway to addressing suffering is to rally our own strength, perhaps we are fortunate to gain some encouragement from others close to us, and we endure the journey with the hope that we will somehow continue to grow stronger through the experience.

As we continue on our journey to build and strengthen our character, it is helpful to highlight another side of suffering. The other side of suffering is an opportunity to grow in empathy towards the suffering of others in order to be a genuine and relevant source of comfort to those in need.

When we walk through the valley of suffering, as opposed to growing bitter or spending too much precious energy on the endless wondering of "why me," we have an opportunity to deeply understand the suffering of others and proactively reach out to help them find comfort in their own troubled time.

There is often no greater connection that can be made with someone suffering through a difficult family experience than one who also has walked through that experience. Those who have endured the financial hardship of a painful bankruptcy are often the most effective in guiding others through the experience of rebuilding their credit and confidence. Who better to support and encourage someone struggling with addiction than someone who has walked down that same road?

Those who have endured a particular hardship are very often the most helpful to relate to the needs of those dealing with a similar struggle. The other side of suffering can be an opportunity to build and strengthen our character and have a positive impact on others when we:

1. Make the choice to grow in empathy towards the suffering of others as opposed to growing bitter through our own experience.

2. Act on an opportunity to make a connection with someone who is enduring a similar struggle to our own.

3. Grow stronger, not just by enduring our own struggle, but also by the truth that being a comfort to others in need grows our own capacity to live a more abundant life.

As we leverage the experience of our own suffering to help others in need, we build and strengthen our character, and *Character Creates Opportunity* to have a positive impact in this world.

Questions to Dig Deeper

When have I suffered in silence and just tried my best to carry on?

What small step can I take to help someone in their time of suffering?

<u>Weekly Reflections</u>

What have I learned and/or how have I grown in the prior week?

_____

_____

What are my hopes for the week ahead?

_____

_____

What three things am I thankful for that could be a source of encouragement to me in the week ahead?

(1) _____

(2) _____

(3) _____

How am I serving and sacrificing in the important areas of my life?

Family and Friends: _____

_____

Work: _____

_____

Community: _____

_____

What small steps can I take this week to continue to build and strengthen my character?

In my thoughts:

_____

In my decisions:

_____

In my actions:

_____

11

THE LIST THAT MATTERS

We can all use a little help in making the really big decisions in life. Benjamin Franklin is recognized as one of the wisest men in our nation's history. He is known for a method of decision making that has been widely used throughout the world. Essentially, Franklin's process is a matter of drawing a line down the middle of a piece of paper, listing the pros and cons, reflecting on them, and then making a decision.

As we continue on our journey to build and strengthen our character, it is important that we determine what list we bring out when we face difficulties and need to make a decision. These are times when we just can't take Yogi Berra's advice; "When you come to a fork in the road, take it." In reality, when we face challenges and need to make a difficult decision, there are two lists we bring out to help guide our decision.

The **FIRST List** is the one that energizes and encourages us. It reminds us of the times when we actually accomplished something special. The times we received that fortunate break, the positive direction from a close friend, and the help we needed. It reminds us of the blessings of a good start, of being born at a great time, in a land of freedom and opportunity. This list reminds us of the nice things that people say about us. This list speaks to us about our growth and potential.

The **SECOND List** is the one that drains and discourages us. It reminds us of those nagging challenges in our lives that we continually face. This list highlights the troubles in our family and the hurtful, personal attacks we have felt in our lives. This list shows the people around us who seem to get all the breaks and live at the corner of "lucky" and "easy" streets. This list reminds us of the times we have been misunderstood and got the short end of the stick. This list speaks to us about our disappointments and regrets.

The reality for all of us is that at every major decision point, family challenge, or workplace event, we have a choice as to which list we review. We will read it, review it, ponder over it, and we will rely on it to decide what to do next. The choice is ours to make and whether we acknowledge it or not, we make this decision all the time.

Here are a few reasons why the **FIRST List** should be the only one that matters:

1. There is a ton of scientific research and practical life experience that would recommend "count your blessings, name them one by one" really does work in elevating our level of performance, maintaining mental and emotional health, and reaching our goals. There is too much proof to disregard the importance of reminding ourselves of the list of blessings in our lives when we face difficult and challenging situations.

2. We cast a shadow on those around us, whether we accept it or not. When we choose from the Second List, we often drag that attitude around for a while and it has the potential to bring down those around us who we care about most. We all are in a position of influence and it is not a kind thing to do when we bring a dark cloud over others based on our reliance on our Second List.

Every point of transition and decision offers clear opportunities to learn and grow. They are not dead-ends to remind us that we have limits. We are not mice running in the proverbial walled box looking for cheese and no chance for freedom. Each fork in the road opens up a new opportunity to learn, grow, and reach our potential.

As we read from the **FIRST List** and crumple up the Second List, we choose hope, courage, and opportunity. When we base our decisions on the **FIRST List**, we build and strengthen our character, and *Character Creates Opportunity* for us to reach our potential and have a positive impact on those around us.

Questions to Dig Deeper

What "List" have I been reading from lately?

What small step can I take to read more from the **First List** and minimize the Second List?

Weekly Reflections

What have I learned and/or how have I grown in the prior week?

_____

_____

What are my hopes for the week ahead?

_____

_____

What three things am I thankful for that could be a source of encouragement to me in the week ahead?

(1) _____

(2) _____

(3) _____

How am I serving and sacrificing in the important areas of my life?

Family and Friends: _____

_____

Work: _____

_____

Community: _____

_____

What small steps can I take this week to continue to build and strengthen my character?

In my thoughts:

_____

In my decisions:

_____

In my actions:

_____

12

THE QUIET OF THE MORNING

As we move fully into the fall season, the quiet of the morning is much more noticeable than the early rising sun and chirping birds of summer. With the time change that will be coming soon, the dark and quiet early mornings afford all of us the opportunity to reflect on the learnings of the past and prepare for what lies ahead.

In the busyness of life, we often fail to take a moment to reflect on where we have been and briefly remind ourselves where we desire to go in order to build our energy to continue the journey. The quiet of the morning brought on at this time of year supports the chance for some meaningful reflection to help us reach our hopes and dreams.

As we continue on our personal journey to build and strengthen our character, there is an opportunity in the quiet of the morning to reflect on day-to-day happenings and also on the big questions about what we desire to see in the years to come.

The Book of Proverbs says, "Where there is no vision, the people will perish."

Real world experience and academic research would reinforce the importance of determining clear goals and specific plans to achieve those goals in order to make meaningful progress on any endeavor. In addition, psychologists would describe something called "purposeful imagination." Basically, if we can clearly see ourselves achieving those goals, emotionally feel what we would feel like in achieving those goals, and we build strength to endure the inevitable challenges we will face in achieving our goals.

We hear a great deal about "vision" and "purpose" statements for individuals, families, and organizations. These are very powerful tools to focus effort and rally a group to a cause. Many times, with the effort to hang a vision statement on a wall, we fail to reconnect consistently to that statement and over time, our direction drifts off course.

There is a significant opportunity to use the quiet of the morning to reflect on where we have been and where we desire to go, both today, and in the long journey of life.

When we take the time to look forward 5, 10, or 20 years, what do we see?

What is the state of our closest relationships? Do we see relationships that have endured the inevitable ups and downs and continue to strengthen a mutual commitment to each other? Do we see children who are productive members of the family, the community, and the workforce? What is the legacy we leave behind to those who matter most?

What is the impact we are having over the years?

We all should work to develop the habit of consistently making time to reflect on the big questions of life. Take a walk, sit outside, or just briefly look off in the distance during a slow period of a child's practice to see what we truly desire to see in the years to come.

As we take the time to reflect on where we have been and where we desire to go, we will build energy to persevere on our journey and we will continue to build and strengthen our character, and *Character Creates Opportunity* for us to not only see the future we desire, but make meaningful progress towards achieving it.

Questions to Dig Deeper

When was the last time I spent time thinking about my future?

What small step can I take to ensure I am living today to reach the future I desire?

<u>Weekly Reflections</u>

What have I learned and/or how have I grown in the prior week?

_____

_____

What are my hopes for the week ahead?

_____

_____

What three things am I thankful for that could be a source of encouragement to me in the week ahead?

(1) _____

(2) _____

(3) _____

How am I serving and sacrificing in the important areas of my life?

Family and Friends: _____

_____

Work: _____

_____

Community: _____

_____

What small steps can I take this week to continue to build and strengthen my character?

In my thoughts:

In my decisions:

In my actions:

13

A MORE EFFECTIVE QUESTION

"Did you close the sale?" "Did you pass the test?" "Did you win the game?" "Did you complete the project?" "Did you make any money on this idea?"

These are all practical and meaningful questions commonly asked in the home, business, and community.

When our children were younger we would at some point over dinner or before bedtime ask them, "What did you learn today?" When they were young, the answers were filled with new observations of the world, facts from school, and insights from friends. For some reason, asking that to our children now in college and high school gets a glare like we have two heads or something.

However, one of the more thoughtful, caring, and effective questions we can ask ourselves and others is, "What did you learn?"

As we look to continue on our journey to build and strengthen our character, reinforcing the importance of individual and shared learning will enable all of us to more effectively continue along a path to reach our full potential.

There is no doubt that the task needs to be completed, money needs to be made, the student needs to pass the test, and winning leads to championships, but it is the learning that builds the foundation for greater impact down the road.

By reprioritizing our discussion to first ask about learning and second ask about the specific result, we accomplish several critical elements to ensure we remain on a productive path to reach our full potential. Emphasizing learning before accomplishment helps to:

1. Reinforce personal growth, and continual, personal growth is the foundation for building a brighter future for us as individuals and for our family, business, and community.

2. Lessen the risk of getting arrogant with great accomplishments while bolstering our ability to remain humble...we always have more to learn, no matter how accomplished we have become.

3. Demonstrate to others we care more about them than the awards on their wall. Ensuring others know that we care far more about them rather than what they have accomplished, we will keep the door open to genuine, healthy, and meaningful relationships.

4. Encourage others to pursue their dreams rather than live in a box defined by the expectations of others. Moving out from under the expectations of others will enable all of us to take greater responsibility for our choices, more fully realize our strengths and weaknesses, develop clarity around our true purpose, and live a life with fewer regrets in the end.

As we continue to place an emphasis on learning, we will build and strengthen our character, and our *Character Creates Opportunity* to continue to grow, reach our full potential, and be an encouraging voice to those around us.

Questions to Dig Deeper

Do I spend more time focused on completing the task or on what I learned?

What small step can I take to ensure I learn and grow while I complete a task?

Weekly Reflections

What have I learned and/or how have I grown in the prior week?

_____

_____

What are my hopes for the week ahead?

_____

_____

What three things am I thankful for that could be a source of encouragement to me in the week ahead?

(1) _____

(2) _____

(3) _____

How am I serving and sacrificing in the important areas of my life?

Family and Friends: _____

_____

Work: _____

_____

Community: _____

_____

What small steps can I take this week to continue to build and strengthen my character?

In my thoughts:

_____

In my decisions:

_____

In my actions:

_____

14

WHEN WE WERE CHILDREN

No, this is not an "old school" story about walking up hill in the snow both ways to school and how tough it was compared to today's children. Rather, it is a note about what we believe.

When we were children, we were "believers." We believed in the impossible and we believed it when others said we had great potential and could accomplish great things. Sure, we also may have believed in the boogeyman and monsters under our bed, but we believed in our potential to do great things.

It may have been a parent teaching us how to ride a bike, shoot a basket, or finish a difficult math problem. It may have been a coach preparing us for the big game or just a tough practice. It may have been a friend who was the "adventurer" and helped us believe. When we were children, someone helped us to believe we had unlimited potential.

There was a time when we believed it. When we believed in ourselves to achieve great things.

Then something happened.

Someone told us we couldn't do it and we believed their limitations. We may have fallen short one too many times. We may have grown callous to hope through time and experience.

As we continue to build and strengthen our character, we need to face the reality of what has impacted our ability to believe in ourselves and take the necessary steps to believe again.

When we strip away all the fluff, there is the reality of a few key areas that are at the foundation of how we became a non-believer:

- **Fear.** We all carry with us some fear. Fear of failure, humiliation, going hungry, of being alone, etc. Fear unchecked can cause us to be unbelievers. Fear as adults most often resembles the monster under our bed. Our fear of whatever, many times does not come about and if it does, it is rarely as bad as it seems…just like the monster under our bed.

- **Negativity.** We finally gave in to the negative view that most often surrounds us. Psychologists say it takes most of us about 5 positive affirmations to overcome one negative opinion. Often times, we have become overwhelmed by the negativity and slowly we moved down the path of no longer believing in our potential. Like the character in *The Sun Also Rises* when asked how did you go bankrupt? "Gradually and then suddenly," our emotional bank account just got too far in the negative that we have felt bankruptcy was our only option.

- **Choice**. We make the choice to believe or not to believe. We can pass the buck if want to, but the truth is, we own the choice and at some point, we chose not to believe.

Here are a few ideas to reconnect with our childhood and become believers again in order to reach our full potential:

- **Faith**. We all have faith. Whether it is faith in God, ourselves, our family, the truth contained in the natural law of the harvest (we reap what we sow), we all have faith that the sun will come up this morning and we face a new day. Don't lose faith.

- **Positive reinforcement.** Whether we describe it as counting our blessings, stopping to smell the roses, or taking some inventory of our past accomplishments, we need reminders of the positives in our life. These small, consistent steps are our most effective way to pay off a huge deficit of negativity in our own emotional bank account.

- **The company we keep**. Often times, we become like those around us. Seek out the relationships that combine a view of the world that is realistic and favors the side of positive and is full of opportunity vs. negative and full of doom and gloom. When our closest, committed relationships have a negative bent, maintain the effort to stay on the positive and our influence will be felt over time.

When we were children, we were believers. It may be time for each of us to relearn the importance of believing in our potential to achieve the healthy goals we desire like strong, loving relationships, productive employment to make a positive difference in the marketplace and the home front, and those really BIG dreams that many times we have kept to ourselves.

As Teddy Roosevelt believed, "Far better it is to dare mighty things, to win glorious triumphs, even though checkered by failure, than to take rank with those poor spirits who neither enjoy much nor suffer much because they live in the gray twilight that knows neither victory nor defeat."

It is time to become believers again and step back into the ring.

As we make the choice as adults to believe again, we will continue to build and strengthen our character, and *Character Creates Opportunity* to reach our full potential and have a great impact on those around us.

Questions to Dig Deeper

When do I let negativity and fear impact my thinking?

What small step can I take to consistently reinforce a positive belief in myself?

Weekly Reflections

What have I learned and/or how have I grown in the prior week?

_____

_____

What are my hopes for the week ahead?

_____

_____

What three things am I thankful for that could be a source of encouragement to me in the week ahead?

(1) _____

(2) _____

(3) _____

How am I serving and sacrificing in the important areas of my life?

Family and Friends: _____

_____

Work: _____

_____

Community: _____

_____

What small steps can I take this week to continue to build and strengthen my character?

In my thoughts:

_____

In my decisions:

_____

In my actions:

_____

15

THE CHALLENGE TO KEEP SERVING

Throughout the years, there has been a steady amount of academic research, business experience, and personal testimony in support of the concept that when we view our role as serving others, we form a strong foundation from which to create value. Whether we are serving our customers, the teams we work on, members of our family, or people in our community, the idea of serving others helps strengthen our efforts to accomplish great things.

In the service of others, especially in the home, we have a clear opportunity to meet our greatest need, which is to know that we matter to someone. Even as we have an abundance of opportunity to meet this need in the home, practical experience would tell us that this need is often met on the job and in the community, given the many conflicts that arise in the home. Since no accomplishment can compensate for a failure at home, the need to sustain an attitude of service in the home is critical.

As we continue on our journey to build and strengthen our character, there is an important paradox in the role of serving others in the home that we need to understand as we genuinely work to meet this important personal need of knowing that we matter to someone.

We have all heard the saying, "opposites attract." It is definitely true in the scientific world and it also seems very common in the human condition when finding a mate. We see the real-life examples of this all around us:

The organizer who is paired with the messy and frantic.

The stable and secure with the chaotic and risky.

The provider being able to help the one in need.

The afflicted and struggling being supported and encouraged to change by the martyr.

We all bring certain strengths to a relationship and we use those strengths in an honest, genuine attempt to serve and help our mate. Most healthy relationships are grounded in serving one another. This heart-felt commitment to serve and support our mate provides the foundation for meeting our deep personal need to know we matter to someone.

Most often, we feel secure in using our strengths to serve our mate because it is a known skill for us and we are confident in our ability to deliver the service and meet the need. We genuinely feel that by serving our mate in this way we will satisfy our own need of being wanted, needed, and appreciated. The general expectation is that our mate will recognize our service and deliver a response that will confirm our need to know we matter.

Because of real practical differences in how we show love and appreciation and in our personalities and communication styles, the *Servant's Paradox™* comes into play in two ways: Many times our mate will (1) Not "see" our intent to serve and will view our efforts as belittling or demeaning and (2) If they do "see" our intent to serve, they will respond in a manner that does not resonate positively with us. The eventual outcome is that we don't feel appreciated and don't meet the need to know we mattered to someone else despite all of our genuine efforts to serve.

With this clear disconnect, frustration eventually sets in. We start to resent those qualities in our mate that we originally intended to use our strengths to serve and help. We quit serving, contempt sets in soon after, and we start talking about "irreconcilable differences" as grounds for a break-up.

The cycle continues as we find another mate with the same gaps as our first and we faithfully try again to serve with a known strength of our own. In addition, even if we endure this disconnect with our mate, the age-old challenge of balancing effort between work and family, the *Servant's Paradox* has a tendency to shift the balance over to work instead of our mate when the need to know we matter is felt greater in the workplace than on the home front.

As we continue on our journey to build and strengthen our character, below are a few steps to take in addressing the *Servant's Paradox* and maintaining the effort to serve:

1. Acknowledge the reality that we all have a need to know we matter to someone.

2. Appreciate the fact that each of us genuinely serves with our strengths to meet the needs of our mate.

3. Be intentional about understanding the different ways our mate feels appreciated in their commitment to serve.

4. Act on the understanding to deliver in a manner that resonates with our mate to meet the need to know they matter in our lives.

5. Keep serving. Serving others is the timeless, universal principle that will not disappoint in the long run. It is the long run that matters.

As we continue to serve and work to effectively recognize the service of others, we will build and strengthen our character, and *Character Creates Opportunity* for us to sustain our efforts to serve others and we stand a great chance to meet our need to know we matter.

Questions to Dig Deeper

In what ways do I serve those closest to me?

What small step can I take to strengthen my commitment to serve those I care about most?

Weekly Reflections

What have I learned and/or how have I grown in the prior week?

_____

_____

What are my hopes for the week ahead?

_____

_____

What three things am I thankful for that could be a source of encouragement to me in the week ahead?

(1) _____

(2) _____

(3) _____

How am I serving and sacrificing in the important areas of my life?

Family and Friends: _____

_____

Work: _____

_____

Community: _____

_____

What small steps can I take this week to continue to build and strengthen my character?

In my thoughts:

_____

In my decisions:

_____

In my actions:

_____

16

WHEN COMMITMENT REMAINS

There comes a point in time in every long-term relationship, every major work endeavor, every pursuit of a life-long dream, and each time we attempt to make a change in our own behavior, when quitting starts to look good. When we question the original choice we made and we look for a way out.

The excitement surrounding the start of a new journey carries us for quite a while and then, when the really hard work begins, our internal voice starts to ask a few questions.

As we continue on our journey to build and strengthen our character, making effective choices when our commitment begins to falter will help us in the journey to reach our full potential.

We all are very familiar with the motivational stories like Abraham Lincoln overcoming numerous personal, business, and political failures before finally becoming President of the United States. We probably all have a few motivational quotes either on a wall or stuffed in some drawer that help to serve as a reminder of what it takes to overcome struggles. We all need good reminders.

Many times, we become enamored by the story and the ultimate outcome. However, more important than the outcome, are the small acts done day by day. The commitment to show up every day is the real strength of the story.

When we commit to a decision, we will have moments (maybe years of moments) when we don't feel like doing it, when we may believe it was a poor choice. But, when our commitment remains day in and day out, the opportunities to learn, grow, and overcome show up also. Just showing up every day is the "wisdom" that gets lost in the popular stories about overcoming.

As we learn and grow, goals will change over time. The situation may require a different set of decisions as we navigate the journey, but what matters is that we climbed back into the ring each and every day, whether we felt like it or not. Just showing up and staying in the game is often what makes all the difference in the world.

Here are just a few points to consider when our commitment begins to falter:

1. We are all in the same boat. Anyone who has ever made a decision to commit to a goal worthy of effort has encountered a moment when quitting looks like an attractive option.

2. Achieving the goal is not the only celebratory moment. What is worth celebrating is the day in and day out commitment to show up and do the work required. Climbing back in the ring each day is worthy of recognition.

3. Opportunity shows up, when we show up. So, more times than not, the most effective choice we can all make is to keep showing up each and every day.

There will be moments when our commitment begins to falter. However, when we make the simple decision to keep showing up, we will gather momentum behind our commitment. We will continue to build and strengthen our character, and **Character Creates Opportunity** to reach our full potential and accomplish the worthy goals we set.

Questions to Dig Deeper

When was the last time that quitting felt like a good option?

What small step can I take to strengthen my commitment to the things that matter most?

<u>Weekly Reflections</u>

What have I learned and/or how have I grown in the prior week?

_____

_____

What are my hopes for the week ahead?

_____

_____

What three things am I thankful for that could be a source of encouragement to me in the week ahead?

(1) _____

(2) _____

(3) _____

How am I serving and sacrificing in the important areas of my life?

Family and Friends: _____

_____

Work: _____

_____

Community: _____

_____

What small steps can I take this week to continue to build and strengthen my character?

In my thoughts:

_____

In my decisions:

_____

In my actions:

_____

17

THE POWER OF REFLECTION

There is no denying that we live in a fast-paced world. Information about world events travels in an instant, products and companies in the marketplace are seemingly disrupted overnight by innovation from all corners of the world, and schedules in our home and communities seem so jammed to capacity that scheduling a meal with friends takes on the complexity of planning a massive military operation.

In this busy world of ours, many times we do need to figure out how to keep pace just as a matter of survival. Ask someone in the taxi business how their life has changed since Uber came to town. Ask someone in the music business how their life has changed since the days of Napster, YouTube, and streaming music. Just mention Amazon.com and most traditional businesses (not just bookstores) start to get anxious.

These events are not just "business" events. These massive, rapid shifts in the marketplace impact homes, families, and communities. It is important that we all figure out how to keep pace with our rapidly changing world just to ensure we can provide the basics for those closest to us.

However, even in our fast-paced world, there is the need for pause and reflection. As a matter of fact, our intentional effort towards making time to reflect on the things that matter most is even more critical in a fast-paced world. As we continue to build and strengthen our character, the power of reflection will provide opportunity to more effectively navigate a world that is moving at light-speed.

"The unexamined life is not worth living" – Socrates

Whether we describe it as prayer, meditation, quiet time, or whatever, the need to make time to consistently reflect on our lives, the relationships we are building, the choices we are making, and the direction in which we are headed is critical to reaching our full potential.

In the busyness of this world, without reflection, we run the risk of heading full steam over the proverbial cliff, climbing the wrong mountain, or unknowingly dismissing those close relationships that we will most certainly regret at some critical moment in the future.

Here are a few thoughts on leveraging the power of reflection to reach our full potential:

1. Be intentional and make a plan. Nothing worthwhile ever gets done when we just "wing it." Sustaining a plan for reflection takes some personal initiative.

2. Be specific and consistent on a time. Some of us are early morning people, some are night owls, and some can tune out the noise in the middle of a busy day to find some time. Just like the research tells us that great, healthy sleep patterns are found with a consistent bedtime and wake-up time, the same is true for strengthening the power of reflection. Find a time that works and stick with it.

3. Be focused on the big picture. In reflective moments, try to move from the day-to-day issues to the longer term big picture thoughts of relationships, areas of service, and legacy building. Reflecting on these items has been shown to build hope even when facing very difficult circumstances in the present.

4. Be prepared to take a few notes. Jotting down a few thoughts and ideas has been demonstrated to be an effective first step in achieving our hopes and dreams in the important areas of our lives.

As we become intentional about finding some time to reflect away from the busy lives we all lead, we will continue to build and strengthen our character and, *Character Creates Opportunity* to reach our full potential and have a positive impact on those around us.

Questions to Dig Deeper

When was the last time I took some time to quietly reflect on my life and relationships?

What small step can I take to ensure I take an adequate amount of time to step away from the busyness and reflect on the important areas of my life?

Weekly Reflections

What have I learned and/or how have I grown in the prior week?

_____

_____

What are my hopes for the week ahead?

_____

_____

What three things am I thankful for that could be a source of encouragement to me in the week ahead?

(1) _____

(2) _____

(3) _____

How am I serving and sacrificing in the important areas of my life?

Family and Friends: _____

_____

Work: _____

_____

Community: _____

_____

What small steps can I take this week to continue to build and strengthen my character?

In my thoughts:

_____

In my decisions:

_____

In my actions:

_____

18

A SEASON OF OPPORTUNITY

For many parts of the country during the fall season, nature's colors are in full display.

Even though most of us are not farmers by trade, we can sense the abundance of harvest time during the fall season.

As we continue to build and strengthen our character, harvest time helps to remind us of an important truth that we have a tendency to forget during the seasons of life. The fall season and the harvest time remind us of the one basic natural law that most directly translates into a relevant, practical, and universal truth necessary to accomplish our hopes and dreams: The Law of the Harvest; simply, you reap what you sow.

The Law of the Harvest is the simplest and most powerful life-transforming principle. Ironically, we need a consistent, steady reminder of its simplicity and truth during the twists and turns of our life's journey.

The Law of the Harvest, in the natural world, is as true as the law of gravity. If you want to reap an abundant harvest of corn or soybeans in the fall, there is only one pathway to follow: The Law of the Harvest. If we asked any farmer 2,000 years ago or one today in the fields of Iowa, we would get the same general response. There are no shortcuts to an abundant harvest. We must spend time in the winter to make a plan and prepare to implement when the spring comes. In the spring, we must prepare the ground and plant the seed. In addition, throughout the spring and summer, we must cultivate the fields through a long growing season. Then, and only then, will we reap an abundant harvest in the fall.

There is no way to take a short cut. We cannot vacation in the spring and summer and then jam an entire growing season into September. There is no way to pay for the "Speed Pass" lane on the farm and there is no "Easy" button. The natural Law of the Harvest will always be our judge. Just like the law of gravity governs our eventual return to the ground no matter how high we jump, the Law of the Harvest governs our ability to produce our most essential food sources for life. In addition, the Law of the Harvest governs our ability to accomplish our most personal hopes and dreams.

If we want healthy relationships with those closest to us, the Law of the Harvest will be our judge. Are we vacationing all spring and summer with the expectation that relationships will be fine when tough times hit (friendly reminder…the tough times will hit)? Or are we doing the hard work today that looks like sacrifice, selfless service, and the humility to listen and learn?

In our own personal development, the Law of the Harvest will always be our most steady path to lasting growth and accomplishment. If we want a more fulfilling career path, then we need to be intentional about making a plan and working the plan. If we are expecting someone in "management" to come and spoon feed us a fulfilling career plan, we may be waiting for a long time. If we want to maintain our physical, mental, emotional, and spiritual health, we need to make a plan and work the plan. Lasting health is built over time. The Law of the Harvest reminds us that there is no such thing as an overnight success in reaching our hopes and dreams.

Despite our best efforts to adhere to the Law of the Harvest, there is the occasion when it just does not work out. Sometimes a storm hits and hail or heavy rains ruin a season of work. Similarly, in our personal lives, we can be genuinely giving our best effort to live consistently according to the Law of the Harvest and we experience an unfortunate and tragic end to a season of effort.

Just as on the farm and in our own lives, we do our best to keep moving forward through an unforeseen tragedy and we persevere with our own unique ways of coping through the upcoming winter season. Then, with the return of the next spring, we have another season of opportunity to start again and more often than not, the Law of the Harvest will go our way in the next season on the farm and in our lives.

In the most important areas of our lives, it is time to ask a most direct question, "Are we preparing to reap an Abundant Harvest?" In our character…marriage…parenting…friendships…careers…community?

We reap what we sow

I hope we can all use the fall season as a moment of support and encouragement to apply the law of the harvest to achieve our hopes and dreams. As we become intentional about living according to the Law of the Harvest, we will build and strengthen our character, and *Character Creates Opportunity* to achieve our goals no matter what our present situation.

Questions to Dig Deeper

What type of harvest do I expect to reap in my closest relationships?

What small step can I take to ensure I reap an abundant harvest in my relationships that matter the most?

Weekly Reflections

What have I learned and/or how have I grown in the prior week?

_____

_____

What are my hopes for the week ahead?

_____

_____

What three things am I thankful for that could be a source of encouragement to me in the week ahead?

(1) _____

(2) _____

(3) _____

How am I serving and sacrificing in the important areas of my life?

Family and Friends: _____

_____

Work: _____

_____

Community: _____

_____

What small steps can I take this week to continue to build and strengthen my character?

In my thoughts:

_____

In my decisions:

_____

In my actions:

_____

19

REMAINING RELEVANT

"You can't teach an old dog new tricks." "You are out of touch with today."

When facing the speed of change in our homes, the marketplace, and our community, we all have probably heard, said, or thought these phrases on more than one occasion. Typically, as individuals get set in their ways, either in a job or in their home life, the phrase, "You can't teach an old dog new tricks" is said to address a personal shortcoming or to rationalize another person's response to something new and different. The normal dialogue back and forth between generations typically results in someone in a younger generation responding to an older person, hopefully as respectfully as possible, with "You are out of touch with today."

As we continue on our journey to build and strengthen our character, ensuring we remain relevant to those around us will help us have a positive impact on others for many years to come. There are two principles that can help all of us remain relevant to those around us as we continue on our journey: (1) We need to *remain teachable* throughout life and (2) We need to *remain open* to learn from anyone by minimizing the barrier of prejudgment.

Remain Teachable:

There is no denying the fact that our world continues to grow in complexity.

The issues we face in many areas of our lives will not be effectively addressed with the techniques that worked a few decades or even a few years ago. We need to find more effective ways to deal with our reality.

The pace of change in most of our markets is lightning fast and business leaders need to continue to seek improved solutions to add greater value in order to remain relevant. In our homes, whether it is managing our finances, maintaining a strong marriage, or being a more effective parent, our environment continues to grow in complexity and many times we are trying to navigate in uncharted waters. The principles of love, understanding, compassion, etc. are timeless and will always remain relevant. However, how we deliver on those principles needs to adjust with the changing environment.

As we make the choice to remain teachable, we become well positioned to remain relevant to those around us. Blaming someone else, or worse yet, in our own mind saying, "You can't teach an old dog new tricks," will work to weaken our impact.

Remain Open:

In addition to remaining teachable to stay relevant, we need to remain open to understand and learn from anyone. Generationally speaking, the young should remain open to learn from the wisdom of the old and the old should remain open to learn from the new perspective and energy of the young. In addition, diversity of experience, background, gender, race, etc. provide potentially valuable perspectives to understand and learn from.

Both academic research and our own practical experience demonstrate that many times we prejudge the potential teacher with our own thoughts of: "What can we learn from him? He has never worked in our industry." "She does not have a degree in this particular field, what could she possibly teach us?" "He is an old man, there is no way he can relate to what I am dealing with." "She is only a teenager, what could she share that would change what we already know?"

Diversity provides a great foundation for learning. Many times, we prejudge diversity of thought or expression and quickly close the door to learning from others. Making the choice to remain open and willing to learn from others who may appear "different" than us will help us remain relevant to those around us.

Prejudging people because they are "different" or allowing ourselves to fall into "group-think" that quiets their voice, will work to weaken our character and hinder us from reaching our full potential.

As we work to remain teachable and remain open to learn from others, not just those who look and act like us, are from our generation, or share a similar set of life experiences, we will continue to build and strengthen our character, and our *Character Creates Opportunity* for us to remain relevant to those around us and continue to have a positive impact in our life's journey.

Questions to Dig Deeper

In what areas of my life do I remain open to new ideas?

What small step can I take to ensure I continue to learn and remain relevant?

Weekly Reflections

What have I learned and/or how have I grown in the prior week?

_____

_____

What are my hopes for the week ahead?

_____

_____

What three things am I thankful for that could be a source of encouragement to me in the week ahead?

(1) _____

(2) _____

(3) _____

How am I serving and sacrificing in the important areas of my life?

Family and Friends: _____

_____

Work: _____

_____

Community: _____

_____

What small steps can I take this week to continue to build and strengthen my character?

In my thoughts:

_____

In my decisions:

_____

In my actions:

_____

20

THE FINISH LINE

We all like a good race. Whether it is the 100-meter dash, the NYC Marathon, the Kentucky Derby, or a NASCAR race. It is exciting to see the race and how participants cross the finish line. There is a clear start and a clear finish.

As we continue on our journey to build and strengthen our character, it is important that we acknowledge the truth that there is no finish line concerning the important things in life like family, work, finances, and areas of service. Even in death, our legacy carries on to impact those left behind. We have to be careful to avoid the illusion of a finish line to our efforts.

There is a risk to reaching our full potential when we allow ourselves to establish some phantom finish lines that will determine our mindset and our effort. We have probably all found ourselves at one time or another saying something like:

- When I reach a certain income level, then I can get ahead of the bills and things will be ok.

- When the kids get out of diapers, then we will have some time and energy and things will be ok.

- When I get through this busy season, then I will have some time to re-connect with my spouse and our relationship will be ok.

- When I lose these 10 pounds, then I will feel better and things will be ok.

- When I reach a certain career milestone, then there won't be as much stress and things will be ok.

- When I get this degree completed, then I can get my life in order and things will be ok.

It is healthy to establish goals/milestones along the way to assess our progress, but there is a clear difference between a milestone achievement and a finish line ending the race to reach our full potential.

The reality is our journey through life is a lot like the business model of the software industry. We launch with the 1.0 version. We get out there in life, learn some things, see some new opportunities, and realize we didn't plan for everything. We then proceed to make a few improvements and then launch the 2.0 version…then 3.0, and we know how the story continues.

The illusion is that the next version will be the lasting version and will be all we need. Life continues to present us with new opportunities to learn and grow. On the journey to reach our full potential, there is no final version. We will continue to build skills and grow in wisdom and perspective.

If we don't learn and grow, we miss our opportunity to maximize our impact on those things we care about most.

As we make the choice to live fully in the moment with the humility to know we are never done learning and growing, we will continue to build and strengthen our character, and **Character Creates Opportunity** for us to have a positive impact on those closest to us and in service to causes bigger than ourselves.

Questions to Dig Deeper

In what areas of my life am I still focused on a finish line?

What small step can I take to ensure I focus on the journey and not just the finish line of a certain event?

<u>Weekly Reflections</u>

What have I learned and/or how have I grown in the prior week?

_____

_____

What are my hopes for the week ahead?

_____

_____

What three things am I thankful for that could be a source of encouragement to me in the week ahead?

(1) _____

(2) _____

(3) _____

How am I serving and sacrificing in the important areas of my life?

Family and Friends: _____

_____

Work: _____

_____

Community: _____

_____

What small steps can I take this week to continue to build and strengthen my character?

In my thoughts:

_____

In my decisions:

_____

In my actions:

_____

21

SERVICE BEYOND THE SPOTLIGHT

There is a great deal of material written about and attention given to leaders. One of the burdens of leadership is often summarized in the phrase "It is lonely at the top." There are many times when a leader needs to step forward and decide. The leader has gathered all the input, sorted through the data, and then at some point a decision needs to be made. There is that moment of decision when the burden is only fully felt by the leader. This is when a leader confronts that cold reality that it truly is "lonely at the top."

However, today's message is not about the "leader," but about the often-underappreciated role that most of us play…The role of serving to get the job done. Mostly out of the spotlight, behind the scenes, and without the typical fanfare that comes with the lonely role at the top. Similar to an offensive lineman blocking for a great running back or providing protection for a great quarterback to find the open receiver, many of us do our job faithfully day in and day out without being in the spotlight.

As we continue to build and strengthen our character, the commitment to keep moving forward in the quiet role of service to a cause bigger than ourselves will set a positive example for others to follow.

Although many times underappreciated, there is something extremely honorable about the commitment of those who get the job done in our workplace, our communities, and our homes. A tremendous example is quietly set by those getting up on a cold, dark morning and getting the job done on a consistent basis that is worthy of appreciation, but so often goes without it. It does not matter what role we play; whether we get up and load boxes into a truck, pack a lunch for children, sit and hold grandchildren, or plan the strategy for an organization. The day in day out choice we make to get up and get going despite going underappreciated for not just days, but perhaps years, is worthy of praise and honor.

Truth be told, our most underappreciated examples of honorable, quiet service most often occur with those closest to us in our homes and extended family.

We may not realize it, but those around us, whether they are our children, our coworkers, or our neighbors are all impacted by our example to serve. Individuals in high-level positions often earn praise, as well as criticism, for their service by the media. However, the day-to-day example of those in quiet service beyond the spotlight to a cause bigger than themselves and honorably fulfilling their commitments are to be given the highest praise for their impact is positive and lasting on those around them.

All of us, at certain points in our journey across the various roles we play, will feel underappreciated for our efforts. Whether it is an insensitive spouse, a young adult going through that "know it all" phase, a preoccupied boss, or selfish coworkers, we all will go through times of service where we just feel underappreciated.

In most cases, especially in the home, the tide does eventually turn. The insensitive spouse or the "know it all" young adult eventually has that "light-bulb" moment when they realize the quiet service that has been delivered faithfully over the years. However, if they do not, it is important that we do not lose our drive to deliver on our commitments to do our job and fulfill our obligations. Continuing to move forward in quiet service is the right thing to do.

If you have felt underappreciated for a while, take this writing as a little "pat on the back" of encouragement for a job and an example well done. In addition, we all should do some self-reflection and see if we are that insensitive spouse, "know it all" young adult, preoccupied boss, or selfish co-worker and start today to put forth some encouragement and recognition to those who are in honorable, quiet service around us.

As we keep moving forward in quiet service out of the spotlight, we will continue to build and strengthen our character, and ***Character Creates***

Opportunity for us to have a positive impact in our world and on those closest to us.

Questions to Dig Deeper

In what areas of my life do I see myself as a quiet servant?

What small step can I take to continue to serve out of the spotlight?

Weekly Reflections

What have I learned and/or how have I grown in the prior week?

_____

_____

What are my hopes for the week ahead?

_____

_____

What three things am I thankful for that could be a source of encouragement to me in the week ahead?

(1) _____

(2) _____

(3) _____

How am I serving and sacrificing in the important areas of my life?

Family and Friends: _____

_____

Work: _____

_____

Community: _____

What small steps can I take this week to continue to build and strengthen my character?

In my thoughts:

In my decisions:

In my actions:

22

A GATEWAY TO GROWTH

Mistakes...We all make them. *Spoiler alert*...We will all continue to make them.

As kids, we make mistakes in the classroom and get red ink all over our assignments. We make a mistake on the field and our opponent scores. We certainly make mistakes with friends and family as we grow during those difficult adolescent years.

As adults, we continue to make mistakes. We make mistakes at work and the business may lose money, manufacture a defective product, or lose a customer. In relationships, we make some big mistakes around promises made and not kept. We speak up when we should shut up and shut up when we should speak up. We make mistakes with our use of time and money.

Whether we are a child or an adult, mistakes hurt.

For most of us, our mindset is to view mistakes as bad and something to avoid. Mistakes are an inevitable part of life. Mistakes are a necessary part of learning. Psychologists and researchers would tell us that almost all of life's learnings come from mistakes.

Mistakes are the gateway to personal growth.

As we continue to build and strengthen our character, learning to more effectively deal with mistakes will help us reach our full potential.

If we are honest with ourselves, the majority of us gravitate towards ease and comfort when things are going well. We only learn and grow through struggles and tough times.

- On the athletic field, we learn a great deal more when we lose, than when we win.

- In school, we learn and grow more when we see red ink on our papers.

- In business, we learn and grow a great deal more when we miss our objectives, than when we hit our numbers.

- In relationships, we have a tendency to take things for granted when there is a sense of harmony and we are only open to learning and growth when doors get slammed, tempers flare, and we reach a breaking point.

When we view mistakes only as bad and something to avoid, we inhibit learning and experimentation, and we suppress new ideas that could potentially trigger breakthroughs in the home, the workplace, and our communities.

Here are just a few thoughts on how we can build and strengthen our character through the unavoidable encounter with mistakes throughout our journey of life:

1. **Commit to Learn**. When we make mistakes, take on the mindset of learning and growth vs. anger and regret. We will make mistakes. As long as we live, we will keep making mistakes. Commit to learn something and keep moving forward.

2. **Commit to Encourage.** When others close to us make mistakes, act to encourage learning and growth versus bringing additional pain. They will most likely experience plenty of personal "pain and suffering" without us adding more salt to the wound. Offering a word of encouragement to learn and grow through a mistake will build trust, avoid shame, and dismantle fear, which will help to strengthen the relationship.

As we begin to view mistakes as opportunities to learn and grow, we will build and strengthen our character, and *Character Creates Opportunity* to improve relationships and achieve the results we desire.

Questions to Dig Deeper

When was the last painful mistake I made?

What small step can I take to focus on learning versus regret when I make a mistake?

Weekly Reflections

What have I learned and/or how have I grown in the prior week?

_____

_____

What are my hopes for the week ahead?

_____

_____

What three things am I thankful for that could be a source of encouragement to me in the week ahead?

(1) _____

(2) _____

(3) _____

How am I serving and sacrificing in the important areas of my life?

Family and Friends: _____

_____

Work: _____

_____

Community: _____

_____

What small steps can I take this week to continue to build and strengthen my character?
In my thoughts:

_____

In my decisions:

_____

In my actions:

_____

23

THE SILENT TEMPTATION

Our world is full of temptation. The temptations of fame, fortune, and friends with benefits are all around us. In addition, there is a world of temptations to relieve the pain of physical ailments, the emotional trauma of relationship struggles, and the anxiety developed out of today's hyper-stressed environment to have it all.

Many of these temptations, and the individuals who get overwhelmed by them, are well documented in the media and if we are paying close attention, seen around the kitchen table in our homes.

However, the most damaging temptation is the one we keep to ourselves. The silent temptation that is the genesis of so much heartache, pain, and personal struggle is the temptation to compare ourselves to others. In our own silent world of comparing ourselves to others, we lose our own identity. Over time, we struggle to find direction and we often miss our true purpose and passion to reach our full potential.

As we continue on our journey to build and strengthen our character, it is important that we address what can be called the greatest temptation we will face, the silent temptation to compare ourselves to others.

Despite how many billions of people inhabit the earth, there is none like you or me. Whether we believe in the scientific rationale, a faith in an all-mighty God, or both, there is no denying the fact that we are uniquely created. There are no two people in this world that are the same.

It is not just physical differences, but also our experiences and how we see the world as a result of those experiences that makes us unique. There is no value in making a judgment of better or worse about these experiences and points of view. There is tremendous value in acknowledging and valuing our own individual differences and the differences of those around us.

When we give in to the silent temptation of comparing ourselves to others, we begin to diminish the strength of our uniqueness.

- When we silently judge our self-worth based on a relative scale of those around us, we diminish the strength of our uniqueness.

- When we silently rate our home-life based on what we see in the homes of others, we diminish the strength our unique family environment.

- When we silently assess our career based on others, we diminish the strength of our unique learning journey.

Our greatest risk in this world is that we fall short of our potential. Becoming overwhelmed with the temptation to compare ourselves to others is the gateway to a life that falls short of its potential.

When we give in to the silent temptation to compare ourselves to others, we chase a moving target as opposed to remaining fixed on reaching our own unique potential. We would be much more effective in setting a high bar based on our own individual goals and then working hard to achieve our full potential.

As we continue to exercise the discipline to "be me and not you," we build and strengthen our character, and **Character Creates Opportunity** for us to reach our full potential.

Questions to Dig Deeper

In what areas of life do I spend time comparing myself to others?

What small step can I take to focus on reaching my own unique potential instead of comparing myself to others?

Weekly Reflections

What have I learned and/or how have I grown in the prior week?

_____

_____

What are my hopes for the week ahead?

_____

_____

What three things am I thankful for that could be a source of encouragement to me in the week ahead?

(1) _____

(2) _____

(3) _____

How am I serving and sacrificing in the important areas of my life?

Family and Friends: _____

_____

Work: _____

_____

Community: _____

_____

What small steps can I take this week to continue to build and strengthen my character?

In my thoughts:

_____

In my decisions:

_____

In my actions:

_____

24

TRANSITIONS – PART I

As we continue on our own personal journey to build and strengthen our character, the topics for the next two chapters will be around the important opportunity for our personal growth that comes in the form of transitions in life. This chapter focuses on transitions in the typical seasons of life. The next chapter focuses on the need to create transition moments in life in order to continue to raise the bar in our personal growth or as a helping hand to get out of a rut we have created during the somewhat steady, routine seasons of life.

Psychologists, counselors, and a fair amount of academic research would indicate that transitions in life can be a major source of stress and anxiety.

As students, there is the stress of transitioning from middle school to high school and high school to college and/or the workplace.

As adults, the transition of single life to married life, married life to life with children, and then the reversal of roles as children transition to take care of aging parents.

In the workplace, we see transitions happen with new leaders joining the team, promotions or downsizing, acquisitions, new markets we enter, etc. that all bring about stress and strain in the workplace.

Over a few generations, we have seen our communities in transition from relative safe-havens to places where metal detectors greet us in schools and public buildings and the thought of a child riding a bike across town makes us anxious.

The stress and strain in these transitions is typically unavoidable for most of us.

However, with a slight shift in mindset, these transitions offer tremendous opportunity to grow and reach our full potential. The mindset shift occurs when we acknowledge these simple truths (A) There will be periods of pain and discomfort in all transitions. (B) There is truly no way to turn back the clock to the way things were as life is always moving forward whether we acknowledge it or not. (C) Embracing these inevitable transitions opens a door to reach our full potential.

Once we make this mindset shift, the benefits to our own personal growth and to the positive impact we can have on those around us is tremendous. When we are intentional about learning and growing through these typical transitions in life we will:

1. **Gain a broader perspective.** As we transition through new experiences, we develop a greater understanding of other people's points of view, experiences, and approaches, which expands our thoughts and improves our decision-making ability.

2. **Build resilience and strength for the future**. Life will never be free of transitions. We can have confidence in knowing that as we grow through this current transition, we will become stronger and more resilient to deal with the next challenge in our journey.

3. **Get a chance to push the "reset" button**. Let's face it...we all make mistakes. When we walk through these major life transitions, we are afforded the opportunity to "start again" with the benefits of past learnings to guide us to more effective choices in our new roles and relationships.

In dealing with the typical transitions in life, the choice is ours. We can go "kicking and screaming" through these transitions, or we can embrace the chance to build and strengthen our character and realize the truth that *Character Creates Opportunity* to reach our full potential.

Questions to Dig Deeper

What were some difficult transitions in my life?

What small step can I take to focus on the benefits of the next transition?

<u>Weekly Reflections</u>

What have I learned and/or how have I grown in the prior week?

_____

_____

What are my hopes for the week ahead?

_____

_____

What three things am I thankful for that could be a source of encouragement to me in the week ahead?

(1) _____

(2) _____

(3) _____

How am I serving and sacrificing in the important areas of my life?

Family and Friends: _____

_____

Work: _____

_____

Community: _____

_____

What small steps can I take this week to continue to build and strengthen my character?

In my thoughts:

_____

In my decisions:

_____

In my actions:

_____

25

TRANSITIONS – PART II

The previous chapter focused on how the typical transitions in life can be great opportunities for personal growth. When we are intentional about learning and growing instead of resisting change through these often difficult transitions, we find ourselves on an effective path to reach our full potential.

For most of us, the typical transitions in life come about by just following the crowd in the routine choices of life. The student transitions through school years and then into the workforce. The transitions into marriage, children, and caring for aging parents all somewhat follow the flow of the typical journey of our modern life. As we discussed in the previous chapter, these transitions can be difficult, but they also afford us a tremendous opportunity for personal growth.

The focus of this chapter is on how we can identify and create transition moments in life in order to "raise the bar" in our personal growth and to provide a helping hand in getting out of a rut we have created during times we have become comfortable, settled, and perhaps a bit complacent.

We have all heard the simple truth that "life is a journey, not a destination." However, for most of us, it is those destination points in life (graduation, a good job, a family, a role in service to others) that pose our greatest risk of becoming complacent and settled. Our mindset becomes "I have worked hard, persevered through challenges, learned, and 'arrived.' Now I can take my foot off the gas and coast for a bit." We all know that mindset is a recipe for disaster in the workplace, in maintaining a marriage, raising children, and in any other meaningful role we may play in life.

Instead of getting stuck in a rut or risking a disaster in an area of life that we genuinely care about, how can we maintain a desire for personal growth during the routine seasons of life and mimic the opportunity to grow that we find during major transition points in life?

Here are a few suggestions:

1. **Accept the Reality** that our current status (a good job, a committed marriage, emotionally healthy children) is at risk if we are not intentional about our own growth. Will Rogers said it best, "Even if you are on the right track, you'll get run over if you just sit there." We are at risk the moment we feel we "arrived" on the fresh side of a typical transition point in life.

2. **Clarify Intentions**. It is important that we clearly decide what we want to become and how we want to act in the many roles we play. "Winging it" sounds cool on the dance floor, but in the really important things in life, we will fall way short of our potential without being intentional with our efforts.

3. **Leverage the natural rhythms of life** as fresh starts to make incremental changes to improve. Routine points in the year like the start of summer break, going back to school, the New Year, anniversaries, birthdays, holidays, even "Mondays" can be extremely practical and relevant times to declare a fresh start on making a small, incremental change to reach a new goal.

4. **Sustainability**. For many of these typical transition points in life, we are in it for the long haul. We don't start and then stop being a parent, or being a son or daughter, and most of us will be "working" at something throughout our lives. Marriages, well sometimes that may be a different story, but our original intention is to be in it for the long haul. We have all probably experienced times when we tried to make massive changes in some area of our lives after attending a "pump-up" motivational event, "re-dedicated" our efforts to something, or a genuinely significant life event (sickness, family break-up, job loss, etc.) caused us to "wake up" and try to get on the right track. The data would demonstrate that massive life changing plans usually are not sustainable for any of us over the long haul.

What seems to work best is making small, incremental change over time that builds momentum for us to sustain heading in the right direction over the long haul. Decide on small changes and start making progress.

5. **The Crowd We Keep**. We often tell our kids how important it is that they hang out with the "right" crowd, not the "wrong" crowd, because for most of us, we follow the crowd. As adults, we don't always take our own advice. We should seek to connect with those who are encouraging and supportive of heading down an effective path vs. those who bring negativity and apathy on any path. Find the "right" crowd and stick with them, just like we tell our kids.

Like most things in life, the choice is ours. We can become set in our ways and find we have created a rut or worse a coffin that limits our potential. Or we can ignite a spark of change during the routine seasons of life, so we can continue to grow and reach our full potential. As we decide to continue to move forward in growth, we build and strengthen our character and realize the truth that *Character Creates Opportunity* to reach our full potential and make a positive impact on those around us.

Questions to Dig Deeper

In what areas of life do I feel stuck or set in my ways?

What small step can I take to spark change in an area where I feel stuck?

Weekly Reflections

What have I learned and/or how have I grown in the prior week?

_____

_____

What are my hopes for the week ahead?

_____

_____

What three things am I thankful for that could be a source of encouragement to me in the week ahead?

(1) _____

(2) _____

(3) _____

How am I serving and sacrificing in the important areas of my life?

Family and Friends: _____

_____

Work: _____

_____

Community: _____

_____

What small steps can I take this week to continue to build and strengthen my character?

In my thoughts:

_____

In my decisions:

_____

In my actions:

_____

26

I AM AFRAID

When discussing topics around the importance of character, we often hear phrases like, "people just need to do the right thing" or "it is pretty basic, just like the things we learned as young kids in school." In many ways, how we build and strengthen our character is pretty straight-forward.

The vast majority of people would agree that our homes and our world would be in better shape if we lived our lives with integrity, took more personal responsibility, removed bitterness and resentment from our thoughts, focused on serving more than being served, etc. In addition, people finding a career path that truly taps into their strengths and fuels their passions is the most effective way to have a lasting, positive impact in the workplace. Organizations, filled with people who are personally and professionally aligned with the vision and culture of the organization, tend to outperform their dysfunctional peers by a wide margin.

Given the above understanding, the key question to ask is, "Why don't we do it?"

When I reflect on some of my own choices or speak with others about choices they made, there seems to be a common theme. When we cut through all the justification language, the well-articulated rationale, the defensiveness around a decision, etc., more times than not, we are left with some form of *FEAR*, often buried beneath insecurity, that is the force that holds us back from making the most effective choices in our lives.

When we need to have that difficult conversation about an important issue that is hindering the growth of our most precious relationships, we often allow the fear of a potential "bad" outcome hold us back from moving forward. Our mind is filled with thoughts like:

"The last 10 times I tried to have this conversation, it ended up really bad, so just forget it."

"He/she always twists my words around and I can't think fast enough to respond."

"As soon as he/she rolls those eyes at me, I just lose it."

In the workplace, when we need to have those challenging conversations with a boss, a coworker, or an employee, we often allow fear to hold us back with thoughts like:

"If I raise this issue with him, I know it will be the death knell to my career with the company."

"He gets so defensive when I talk about working as a team. Forget it...I will just do it myself."

"The last time I saw someone challenge the boss' opinion, they were 'ripped apart,' so forget about speaking up. I will just deal with it."

Deep down, the truth behind many of our decisions not to "do the right thing" is because of *FEAR*.

Fear has its place in our lives. In some short-term situations like walking at night in a bad part of town, a little fear is good to keep us on high alert. Having a little fear when the doctor says we need to eat better and exercise more may be just what we need to get motivated. Just before we make the decision to buy that new car, take that big vacation, or financially "stretch" into a larger home, a little fear is good to ensure we understand all the potential outcomes before spending the money.

However, in the context of strengthening relationships and pursuing a life of positive impact, it is not healthy to let fear be the driving force behind our thoughts, decisions, and actions. We should put fear in its place as we anchor our decisions on timeless, universal principles like courage, discernment, and discretion to make the most effective choice and do the right thing. Have that difficult conversation, put the issue on the table at work, and pursue the career choice that would be most fulfilling.

There is one practical step we can take to help ensure fear does not have an unhealthy impact on the choices we make. As we walk through the decision-making process and assess the potential positive and negative outcomes of a particular decision, simply ask one additional question:

"If I was not afraid, what would I do?"

Addressing this basic question helps acknowledge the reality that somewhere in the mix of major decisions there is always a little fear and it opens the door to be brutally honest with ourselves as we work through making the decision.

Fear has its place in our lives. As we guide our thoughts, decisions, and actions by principles such as courage, loyalty, and commitment, we build and strengthen our character, and our *Character Creates Opportunity* to help minimize the negative impact of fear in our lives as we pursue our hopes and dreams.

Questions to Dig Deeper

In what areas of life have I let fear guide my decisions?

What small step can I take to ensure fear does not dominate my decisions?

Weekly Reflections

What have I learned and/or how have I grown in the prior week?

_____

_____

What are my hopes for the week ahead?

_____

_____

What three things am I thankful for that could be a source of encouragement to me in the week ahead?

(1) _____

(2) _____

(3) _____

How am I serving and sacrificing in the important areas of my life?

Family and Friends: _____

_____

Work: _____

_____

Community: _____

_____

What small steps can I take this week to continue to build and strengthen my character?

In my thoughts:

_____

In my decisions:

_____

In my actions:

_____

27

TO BE REMEMBERED

For a variety of reasons, most of us will not have our names in the history books, the world-record books, or any other well-known document read by millions in the next 100 to 200 years.

Most of us have a knowledge of and maybe some vivid memories of a few key people in the generations of our past. We certainly can remember parents, grandparents, and perhaps great-grandparents, but it starts to get real fuzzy after a few generations. Depending on our level of engagement with parents and grandparents, we may have memories of their friends, maybe coworkers and bosses, but for all practical purposes, there is limited personal knowledge beyond the family tree when we go back a few generations.

So, there we have it; a practical view of being remembered and leaving a legacy is that we probably have a realistic chance that our grandchildren and maybe our great-grandchildren will remember us. I can remember a great quote from Cal Ripken upon his retirement from baseball, when he was asked, "How do you want to be remembered?" Cal replied, "Just being remembered would be nice." In many ways, a great hope for all of us would be to "just be remembered" by our grandchildren and great-grandchildren.

I doubt any of us can recall whether a great-grandparent wore fashionable clothes, drove the finest car of the day, had a great watch, or some other material possession. At most, we remember, or we were told, whether or not they were involved in their family, in their work, and in service to a cause bigger than themselves. We remember if they were kind and helpful or mean and hurtful.

As we continue on our journey to build and strengthen our character and reach our full potential, it would be great to have a few generations along the family tree not only "just remember us," but remember us as kind, helpful, productive, and committed to our family and to a worthy cause…the things that matter most.

As we think about leaving a legacy, here are a few practical considerations:

- We need to be intentional with our efforts to leave a legacy as there is a great risk of being forgotten. Like many important endeavors, intentional effort begins with a big dream or idea, followed by the very practical steps of making a plan and then the discipline to work the plan. Leaving a legacy within our families is too important to just "wing it."

- No matter what has happened in the past, today is the best day to start fresh and move forward to create the legacy we desire.

- As the saying goes, our thoughts turn into actions; our actions turn into habits; our habits develop our character; and our character becomes our legacy. Leaving a legacy starts in our thought life. When our thoughts, that drive decisions and then actions, are grounded in principles like commitment, loyalty, and sacrifice, we build and strengthen our character and **Character Creates Opportunity** to leave the legacy we all desire.

We only have that great unknown, which is "the rest of our lives," to make progress. Enjoy the journey.

Questions to Dig Deeper

What legacy do I want to leave?

What small step can I take to make progress on building the legacy I desire?

Weekly Reflections

What have I learned and/or how have I grown in the prior week?

_____

_____

What are my hopes for the week ahead?

_____

_____

What three things am I thankful for that could be a source of encouragement to me in the week ahead?

(1) _____

(2) _____

(3) _____

How am I serving and sacrificing in the important areas of my life?

Family and Friends: _____

_____

Work: _____

_____

Community: _____

_____

What small steps can I take this week to continue to build and strengthen my character?

In my thoughts:

_____

In my decisions:

_____

In my actions:

_____

28

THREE IMPORTANT ELEMENTS

Our world continues to grow in complexity, intensity, and uncertainty. Often times, the challenges before us seem increasingly more difficult to address, whether it is building a competitive edge in a global marketplace, maintaining peace and security in our communities, or getting the time and attention to guide and support those individuals we care about most.

Despite the growing complexity in our world, there have been three elements to building a strong foundation that have endured the test of time to help us more effectively address the challenges we face in our world. As we continue on our journey to build and strengthen our character, we can have a positive impact on all three elements.

The three elements to build a strong foundation to more effectively address the challenges in our world are the following:

Family

There has been a tremendous amount of research done on the perils that result with the break-up of the family unit. Families may come in a few different flavors in our world today, but the basic principles of having a "home" where people feel love, support, safety, and commitment is an incredibly solid foundation for making a positive impact in our world, no matter what challenges we face.

As we continue to guide our thoughts, decisions, and actions in the "home" by principles like commitment, loyalty, and grace, we build and strengthen our character and our character creates opportunity to strengthen our family to more effectively address the challenges we face in our world.

Education

Applying effort to continue to learn and grow in school, the workplace, the home, and our community is critical to effectively addressing the growing complexity in our world. Education does not end with graduation day. In many ways, our real education is just beginning. When we refuse to learn and grow with comments like, "that is just the way I am," we set ourselves up to have limited positive impact on those around us.

As we continue to guide our thoughts, decisions, and actions by principles like understanding, humility, and respect, we build and strengthen our character and our character creates opportunity to stay educated and more effectively address the challenges we face in our world.

Economic Opportunity

There is tremendous honor in fulfilling our duty to get out of bed and go to work. That "work" may have us remain in the home, travel to an office, defend our freedom, dig a ditch, or aid the hurting. Regardless of the type of work, work builds and strengthens our character.

There are times in the economic cycle of free markets and in certain communities, where there seems to be limited economic opportunity. However, even in the darkest times, we should be reminded of the reality that Thomas Edison shared a long time ago, "Opportunity is missed by most people because it is dressed in overalls and looks like work."

As we continue to guide our thoughts, decisions, and actions by principles like perseverance, sacrifice, and hope, we build and strengthen our character and our character creates opportunity for us to work to the best of our abilities and more effectively address the challenges we face in our world.

There is limited value in hoping for a more simple and predictable world. A more productive use of our time and effort should be towards building a solid foundation to address the realities of our world today.

As we focus effort on the three elements of family, education, and economic opportunity, we will help to build and strengthen our character, and *Character Creates Opportunity* for us to build a strong foundation to more effectively address the complexity of our world today.

Questions to Dig Deeper

How am I progressing in support of my family, education and economic opportunity?

What small step can I take to raise the bar on my efforts?

Weekly Reflections

What have I learned and/or how have I grown in the prior week?

_____

_____

What are my hopes for the week ahead?

_____

_____

What three things am I thankful for that could be a source of encouragement to me in the week ahead?

(1) _____

(2) _____

(3) _____

How am I serving and sacrificing in the important areas of my life?

Family and Friends: _____

_____

Work: _____

_____

Community: _____

What small steps can I take this week to continue to build and strengthen my character?

In my thoughts:

In my decisions:

In my actions:

29

MAKING PROGRESS

Our world continues to get more challenging. Although we may talk about big goals like improving education, addressing poverty, and eliminating the oppression of certain groups, it is often very difficult to genuinely see and "feel" progress being made in our day-to-day lives.

The purpose of this chapter is to bring a progress check much closer to home, where the potential for global change actually begins and where it matters most.

We are all familiar with the importance of setting goals, building a plan to achieve those goals, and using some date on a calendar like a birthday, the New Year, or the start of school to help jump start the process in a healthy and often convenient way to initiate needed change in our lives. Unfortunately, we are probably also familiar with the reality that the vast majority of us will abandon, or just plain forget, our goals almost as quickly as we set them.

Today's chapter is not about rallying around some collective motivation or new process to more effectively achieve our goals. There is already plenty of information out there to help us all get a little more motivated to achieve our goals.

Today's chapter is about the importance of recognizing small steps of progress along the way in order to keep the momentum going. The "world" (feel free to insert your own relevant term) judges or highlights the finish line. However, most often it will be us alone, in the quiet of the journey, who will be in a position to celebrate making progress in the right direction on the things that matter most.

As we continue on our journey to build and strengthen our character, a helpful discipline we alone can exercise is the personal "high five" we can give ourselves for making progress on the journey to reach our hopes and dreams in matters close to home.

There will be a great deal written about the steps to achieving the common goals of losing weight, exercising or some professional career milestone. However, the real need to celebrate making progress towards often our most challenging goals, which is rarely written or talked about, is in having a positive impact on those closest to us in our homes and families. A helpful discipline is to acknowledge the small steps of progress we make in:

1. Judging less and encouraging more

2. Breaking the cycle of a painful past to bring healing to an important relationship

3. Experiencing the lasting joy of serving and giving instead of the short-term pleasure of getting our way

4. Opening dialogue on an important issue rather than avoiding it

5. Courageously acknowledging our fears and insecurities while minimizing our concern of judgement or shame.

The "world" will celebrate the big achievements in business, politics, entertainment, etc. As we choose to celebrate making progress in the home and with the ones closest to us, we will build the foundation to achieve great things in the marketplace, the community, and our world.

As we make the choice to personally celebrate the small steps of progress we make in our close relationships, we will continue to build and strengthen our character, and **Character Creates Opportunity** for us to bring health into relationships closest to us.

As we continue to clearly define our hopes and dreams in the home, let us not forget that "A journey of a thousand miles begins with a single step" (Lao Tzu). Congratulations, in advance, for the steps of progress you will make with the ones closest to you.

Questions to Dig Deeper

What small steps of progress have I made in things that matter most?

What small step can I take to consistently remind myself of the progress I am making?

Weekly Reflections

What have I learned and/or how have I grown in the prior week?

_____

_____

What are my hopes for the week ahead?

_____

_____

What three things am I thankful for that could be a source of encouragement to me in the week ahead?

(1) _____

(2) _____

(3) _____

How am I serving and sacrificing in the important areas of my life?

Family and Friends: _____

_____

Work: _____

_____

Community: _____

_____

What small steps can I take this week to continue to build and strengthen my character?

In my thoughts:

_____

In my decisions:

_____

In my actions:

_____

30

BOUNCING BACK

Well, I guess we did not win the Powerball lottery last night. Now what do we do?

Well, I guess our plans did not come together like we had hoped. Now what do we do?

Well, I guess our plans to retire after 30 years with the company ended at year 15 with a downsizing exercise. Now what do we do?

Well, I guess our dream of a quiet neighborhood ended when the neighbor's rowdy grandson inherited the house. Now what do we do?

Well, I guess our plan for "happily ever after" is not looking so good. Now what do we do?

Well, I guess our plans for a care-free retirement ended when the kids moved back in. Now what do we do?

Well, I guess our plans to hand down a great family business ended when the "supercenter" came to town. Now what do we do?

The reality of our day-to-day lives is that many things don't come together according to plan. To pull from the wisdom of Ben Franklin, it is really only death and taxes that we can count on.

Resilience is a character trait defined as the ability to bounce back after a setback. As we continue on our journey to build and strengthen our character, building resilience into our personal skill-set would be a most valuable endeavor to reach our full potential.

How do we handle a set-back? Do we take our ball and go home, fold up our tents and walk away, or do we pick ourselves up, adjust our plans with the new set of information, and get back after the goal?

Here are a few things to consider in helping to build and strengthen our resilience:

1. We are not the only ones whose plans fell off the rails and encountered a near term failure. Even the sharp dressed man or woman who sounds so smart, hits rock bottom every once in a while.

2. Work hard to remain humble when things seem to be going great. Humility will help soften the blow when a set-back comes our way…and a set-back will come our way.

3. It is ok to acknowledge the pain. We should all work to build our tolerance for pain and discomfort, but it is ok to admit a major set-back in an important area of life really hurts.

4. We set a helpful example to those we care about most when we demonstrate the ability to bounce back after a set-back. *Set the example…Resilience* may be the most important life-skill we can teach those we care about most.

Our world continues to grow in complexity and uncertainty, and as we continue to develop our resilience in dealing with the inevitable set-backs, we will continue to build and strengthen our character, and *Character Creates Opportunity* for us to reach our full potential and have a positive impact on those around us.

Questions to Dig Deeper

What setbacks have I recently experienced?

What small step can I take to remain resilient in the face of setbacks?

Weekly Reflections

What have I learned and/or how have I grown in the prior week?

_____

_____

What are my hopes for the week ahead?

_____

_____

What three things am I thankful for that could be a source of encouragement to me in the week ahead?

(1) _____

(2) _____

(3) _____

How am I serving and sacrificing in the important areas of my life?

Family and Friends: _____

_____

Work: _____

_____

Community: _____

_____

What small steps can I take this week to continue to build and strengthen my character?

In my thoughts:

_____

In my decisions:

_____

In my actions:

_____

31

PERSONAL SKILLS – PART I

As we continue on our journey to build and strengthen our character, there are two personal skills that throughout history have been critical to ensuring lasting success in building healthy relationships and having a positive impact in our life's effort. The first of these skills will be covered in this chapter and the second will be addressed in the next chapter.

There is one skill that has been proven over and over again to be a stronger predictor of lifelong success than any other, including IQ, social class, formal education, etc. Philosophers in ancient civilizations, the world's major religions, and modern-day psychologists all speak to the importance of building this personal skill in order to best position us to have a life of positive impact.

The personal skill deemed critical is self-control in the form of delayed gratification. Delayed gratification is the ability to resist the temptation for an immediate reward and wait for a later, often greater and more enduring reward.

The personal skill to resist the pull of instant gratification to meet an immediate need by focusing on a longer-term goal is worthy of our attention as we build and strengthen our character.

In the modern era, there were two important studies initiated in the 1960s and 1970s that formally measured the long-term impact of delayed gratification that set in motion numerous repeat studies that have continually proved the importance of this skill to a life of positive impact.

The Dunedin (New Zealand) children's study and the Marshmallow Test conducted at Stanford University.

The children of Dunedin (over 1,000 kids born over a single 12-month period) were studied throughout their school years on numerous skills, including their tolerance for frustration and their ability to concentrate and exercise self-control. They were followed up over 2 decades later and assessed across a series of measurements for health, wealth, relationships, and crime rates.

The Marshmallow Test basically placed 4-year-olds in a room with their favorite treat (in most cases marshmallows). Researchers told the children that they could have one marshmallow right now if they wanted it. However, if they did not eat it until the researcher came back after taking care of a few tasks, they could have two marshmallows. About one third of the kids held off until the researcher came back about 15 minutes later and were rewarded with two marshmallows. The children were followed up decades later and assessed on a number of important aspects of life.

In both seminal studies, the results were clear. The kids who demonstrated the skill of delayed gratification had a lifelong difference in terms of healthy relationships, financial well-being, low crime rates, and a host of other positive outcomes. Self-control, in the form of delayed gratification, proved to be a stronger predictor than any traditional measure.

Studies like the ones at Dunedin and Stanford have been repeated and demonstrated similar outcomes. Today's academics have demonstrated strong evidence in support of the teachings of ancient philosophers and the world's major religions.

The capacity to develop self-control demonstrated by these kids, and the same can be said for adults in the journey to live a life of positive impact, can be summarized in two important areas:

1. The ability to mentally and emotionally disengage from the object of our immediate desire (a marshmallow, my need to be "right" in an argument, protect my reputation, effectively cover my insecurities, etc.)

2. The ability to focus on a larger, longer-term goal (like two marshmallows or a healthy relationship in our home).

In very practical terms for all us, the ability to build healthy relationships starts with (a) our ability to disengage from the strong pull to meet our own immediate selfish desires and (b) our ability to take a deep breath and realize the more significant goal of a healthy, positive, long-term relationship is what we are striving for.

As we put effort into developing our self-control to resist instant gratification and focus on the long-term goals of health in our relationships and having a positive impact on our surroundings, we will continue to build and strengthen our character, and our *Character Creates Opportunity* for us to reach our full potential and set an example for others to follow.

Questions to Dig Deeper

In what part of my life do I struggle with self-control?

What small step can I take to minimize my desire for instant gratification?

Weekly Reflections

What have I learned and/or how have I grown in the prior week?

_____

_____

What are my hopes for the week ahead?

_____

_____

What three things am I thankful for that could be a source of encouragement to me in the week ahead?

(1) _____

(2) _____

(3) _____

How am I serving and sacrificing in the important areas of my life?

Family and Friends: _____

_____

Work: _____

_____

Community: _____

_____

What small steps can I take this week to continue to build and strengthen my character?

In my thoughts:

_____

In my decisions:

_____

In my actions:

_____

32

PERSONAL SKILLS – PART II

Following the previous chapter on the important personal skill of delayed gratification as defined as the ability to resist temptation for an immediate reward and wait for a later, often greater and more enduring award, Part II of this message will focus on another important personal skill.

As we continue on our journey to build and strengthen our character, this second skill also has been shown to be critical to ensuring lasting success in building healthy relationships and having a positive impact in our life's effort. This skill is not as well studied in academia as the "marshmallow test" demonstrating delayed gratification, but this second skill is documented throughout history as being an important personal skill.

Part II of this message addresses the critical skill of *proactive service* – the ability to identify a need and make the choice to take action to meet the need. This skill goes sharply against the "what's in it for me crowd," the "I just want to be happy crowd," and the "I am just in it for the money crowd."

Proactive service is embodied in the quote from President John F. Kennedy at his inaugural address in 1961 when he said, "Ask not what your country can do for you—ask what you can do for your country." For those searching for purpose, proactive service is captured in the words of Mahatma Gandhi who said, "The best way to find yourself is to lose yourself in the service of others."

Proactive service is as much a choice as it is a skill. It is a choice to run towards problems instead of away from them. It is a choice to persevere when our selfish needs of recognition and reward make quitting seem like a

131

really good option because we are not getting what we want from the experience.

Proactively looking for ways to serve has been and will continue to be the hallmark of individuals who leave a legacy that endures by leaving the world a better place than they found it. They are most often not characterized by those who made a great financial reward for their skill of serving others or developing a product that meets a huge market need. Proactive service is most commonly seen in:

1. The home by those who continue to serve others in daily tasks that often go unnoticed and underappreciated for years.

2. The workplace by individuals who raise their hand to help when a young supervisor has been given a big task and by those who stay a little later to ensure the job gets done even when it goes past the time to clock out.

3. The community by individuals who choose to serve in capacities of real need even when they could apply those skills and energy to earn a greater financial reward in some other endeavor.

The examples we see all around us of proactive service are worthy of remembering and teaching to others.

Building a strong foundation of proactive service does not start with questions like "What makes me happy" or "What do I do best." Living a life of proactive service begins with the question, "What needs to be done?" Individuals find purpose and passion in identifying needs and getting busy meeting the needs of others in our homes, our workplace, and our community.

As we make the choice to proactively serve in areas of need, we will continue to build and strengthen our character, and our *Character Creates Opportunity* for us to reach our full potential and leave a legacy that sets an example for others to follow.

Questions to Dig Deeper

In what areas of life do I proactively serve others?

What small step can I take to continue to expand my areas of service to others?

<u>Weekly Reflections</u>

What have I learned and/or how have I grown in the prior week?

_____

_____

What are my hopes for the week ahead?

_____

_____

What three things am I thankful for that could be a source of encouragement to me in the week ahead?

(1) _____

(2) _____

(3) _____

How am I serving and sacrificing in the important areas of my life?

Family and Friends: _____

_____

Work: _____

_____

Community: _____

_____

What small steps can I take this week to continue to build and strengthen my character?

In my thoughts:

_____

In my decisions:

_____

In my actions:

_____

33

TOUCH

The local book stores and web pages on Amazon contain countless resources offering advice on how we can build better relationships. Some are complicated with academic theory and no practical application. Some are just the latest well-packaged marketing effort from some media company and others offer genuine value to those looking for some help in a time of real need.

As we all look to build and maintain healthy relationships in the home, workplace, and community, the importance of touch does not get a great deal of attention in our world and is only now beginning to gain some traction within published, academic research.

As we continue on our journey to build and strengthen our character, an opportunity that we do not want to miss is the positive outcomes that result from touch that can build, strengthen, and heal relationships.

We are all well aware of the physical bonding that happens between a loving parent and a young child. There is a strong body of evidence to suggest that loving, physical contact at the early stages of a child's life are critical to a child's physical, mental, and emotional health. There is a great deal of documentation on the steep rise in infant morbidity and mortality when there is a lack of loving, physical contact during the early development years, which has been seen in orphanages around the world.

The reality is that beyond our infant years, we have a tendency to disregard the emotional and physical benefits that result from touch despite the growing body of research that suggests touch is fundamental to communication, relationships, and overall health. Michelangelo said, "To touch is to give life," and there is growing recognition that touch is our primary means for communicating compassion.

This message is not some weird call to start grabbing each other. However, there are many of us who have grown up in western culture where consistent, supportive touch has been so confined to early childhood that we are missing a key element to build, strengthen, and heal our most important relationships. There are studies that show touch signals safety and trust, which are foundational to healthy relationships. When we take an honest assessment of the relationships we value the most, whether they are struggling or not, we will most likely find we are missing the benefits of a warm, supportive touch on a consistent basis.

This message is not just for the home. Even if we were fortunate to grow up in a home where touch was reinforced throughout our lives in support of healthy relationships, chances are that societal pressures probably got the best of us in school and work where a supportive pat on the shoulder is sometimes considered out of line. Studies have shown that teachers who provide a friendly tap on the shoulder increase student engagement and learning. In my own professional journey, I have seen the benefits that a supportive touch on the shoulder can communicate straight to the heart of an individual that they "belong on the team" and that we will work together to deliver results. It is unfortunate that some foolish, out of hand behavior makes the headlines in work and school which increases our collective resistance to providing the benefits of a supportive, helpful touch.

Below are two considerations with regards to the importance of touch and our character:

1. "An ounce of prevention is worth a pound of cure" (thanks to Ben Franklin). Many of us may be talking and acting in a very supportive and encouraging way in our close relationships. However, statistics will show that for most of us, a consistent, supportive touch is not part of the equation. Given the well-documented benefits to our physical, mental, and emotional health and to the health of the relationship, start being intentional about adding a supportive touch to the mix as it will build relationship strength to help overcome the inevitable challenges that relationships bring throughout life. Start in the home and then build some courage to take it elsewhere.

2. When relationships are struggling, there is most definitely an absence of touch. Whether it is the struggles of a parent-child relationship, the routine friction between spouses, or "the big mistake" that created a fracture between close friends, a close touch seems to be a

distant memory during the struggles of everyday relationships. A warm, loving touch should be part of our tool box to bring healing and health back to the relationship. An authentic, genuine embrace can open the door to health more effectively than words and time. Also, if you happen to be on the receiving end of an embrace to heal a troubled relationship, don't resist; reciprocate the embrace and you will both be better off for the touch.

As we demonstrate the courage to incorporate touch into our most valued relationships, we will build and strengthen our character, and *Character Creates Opportunity* to improve the health of our relationships and set a great example for those around us.

Questions to Dig Deeper

When was the last time I gave a gentle, loving touch to someone I care about?

What small step can I take to bring a gentle loving connection back into the relationships I care most about?

Weekly Reflections

What have I learned and/or how have I grown in the prior week?

_____

_____

What are my hopes for the week ahead?

_____

_____

What three things am I thankful for that could be a source of encouragement to me in the week ahead?

(1) _____

(2) _____

(3) _____

How am I serving and sacrificing in the important areas of my life?

Family and Friends: _____

_____

Work: _____

_____

Community: _____

_____

What small steps can I take this week to continue to build and strengthen my character?

In my thoughts:

_____

In my decisions:

_____

In my actions:

_____

34

A REAL CONCERN

As Labor Day signals the end of summer, we have another seasonal time point that can be helpful to set some goals and build momentum towards reaching our full potential. Unfortunately, just like setting some goals for the New Year, the cold hard statistics would remind us that after just a few short weeks, most of us begin to see those goals fade away and become lost and forgotten. It is not so much that we already reached success or failure, but we basically just stopped caring and moved on.

Measuring success or failure in any endeavor is important. However, as we continue on our journey to build and strengthen our character, a real concern is to address apathy when it creeps into our family, our personal and professional growth, and our community…when we just don't care anymore and don't get engaged, set goals or get after achieving them.

The real concern in life is not that we fell short of our goals or faced repeated failure in our attempts to achieve. The real concern is that we just "checked out" in the major areas of life and just stopped caring.

Apathy rears its ugly head in a number of ways and in a variety of dimensions in our lives:

"I am just burned out" may be the way apathy appears from a career perspective. We get tired of the bureaucracy and red tape of an organization and we just grin and bear it until retirement or something better comes along. It also can appear in the entrepreneurial world when we just grow numb to the concerns of cash flow and bankruptcy risk.

"I am just tired of being miserable and unhappy" may be the way apathy appears in our closest relationships.

"You are now on your own to learn the hard way" may be the way apathy appears in dealing with a rebellious child.

"It is beyond repair" may be the way apathy appears in the challenges we face in our communities. When the challenges become so daunting because of the complexity created by the break-down of the family, generational poverty, lack of positive role models, ineffective public and private interventions, that we just check out with the general loss of hope because of the enormity of the problem.

Throughout our journey of life, we will all face moments when apathy enters our mindset. Here are a few considerations to address the challenge:

1. Recognize it. Be attune to our own thoughts and perceptions when we sense ourselves slipping into "I just don't care anymore."

2. Place a reality check on hopes and dreams. Being on the brink of "I just don't care anymore" forces us to ask the big questions in life about purpose, goals, and what really matters. It gives us a chance to gain perspective on our own desires, clarifies needs versus wants, and helps prioritize what is really important that we need to commit to doing.

3. Take small steps in the direction we need to go with the truth that the meaningful and important things in life are achieved on a long, slow journey. Close relationships and service to a cause greater than our own are never captured in a get-rich-quick scheme.

Our character, that internal voice that guides our thoughts, decisions, and actions can be a strong defense against apathy. As we guide our thoughts, decisions, and actions by principles like perseverance, compassion, understanding, and commitment, we build and strengthen our character, and *Character Creates Opportunity* for us to continue on the journey to reach our full potential.

Questions to Dig Deeper

In what areas of my life have I let apathy creep into my thinking?

What small step can I take to guide my thoughts to protect against feelings of apathy?

<u>Weekly Reflections</u>

What have I learned and/or how have I grown in the prior week?

_____

_____

What are my hopes for the week ahead?

_____

_____

What three things am I thankful for that could be a source of encouragement to me in the week ahead?

(1) _____

(2) _____

(3) _____

How am I serving and sacrificing in the important areas of my life?

Family and Friends: _____

_____

Work: _____

_____

Community: _____

_____

What small steps can I take this week to continue to build and strengthen my character?

In my thoughts:

_____

In my decisions:

_____

In my actions:

_____

35

THE FORTUNE

There is truth in the old adage, "the fortune is in the follow up."

It does not matter whether we are talking about closing a sale, strengthening an important relationship, sticking with an exercise routine, or building a strong community, it is in the follow up where we find the fortune.

We have probably all had the experience of a rush of motivation and positive energy after a great initial encounter:

- A great first meeting with a potential new client

- A motivating speech by a political figure or business leader

- A weekend retreat focused on strengthening a close relationship

- An "altar call" moment in our faith journey

- An infomercial product we purchased for healthy eating and exercise

The reality is that when that initial motivation fades, instead of reaping a fortune in the follow up, we go bankrupt due to lack of follow up.

As we continue to build and strengthen our character, the principle of remaining committed in the follow up will create opportunity for us to reach our full potential.

If we all do an honest self-assessment across important endeavors in our lives, I am sure we can find a few teachable moments where we failed to build a fortune due to lack of follow-up. I can recall failing to follow up on a few specific customer commitments and areas of service outside the home. In addition, the real painful shortfalls are those that have occurred closer to home. Perhaps some of you also can relate to a few times where you missed the fortune because of a lack of follow up.

Here are just a few thoughts on building a fortune:

1. Accept the reality that having a meaningful impact on any endeavor in life is contained in the follow up, not in the start.

2. Any follow up is better than no follow up. Taking smaller steps at a slower pace will still produce a meaningful impact.

3. Unfortunately, we will all still have a few experiences in the future where we will miss out on a fortune due to lack of follow up. We should not be dismayed. We should acknowledge the shortfall and just keep climbing back into the ring to try again.

4. Given the reality of #3 above, we should demonstrate some mercy on those closest to us when they fail to follow up as I am sure we would appreciate the same treatment when we inevitably fall short sometime down the road.

When we consistently follow up after a motivating initial encounter, we will build and strengthen our character, and **Character Creates Opportunity** to build a fortune in our relationships, our businesses, and our communities.

Questions to Dig Deeper

When have I recently failed to follow up on an important commitment?

What small step can I take to be more consistent in following up on commitments?

Weekly Reflections

What have I learned and/or how have I grown in the prior week?

_____

_____

What are my hopes for the week ahead?

_____

_____

What three things am I thankful for that could be a source of encouragement to me in the week ahead?

(1) _____

(2) _____

(3) _____

How am I serving and sacrificing in the important areas of my life?

Family and Friends: _____

_____

Work: _____

_____

Community: _____

_____

What small steps can I take this week to continue to build and strengthen my character?

In my thoughts:

_____

In my decisions:

_____

In my actions:

_____

36

THE COURAGE TO ASK

There is no denying that we have entered into the age of instant access to all types of resources to help us be more efficient and effective. On the personal development side, there are websites that can help us be more efficient with planning schedules, meals, vacations, and just about anything else. There is also no shortage of books or consultants we could employ to help us in everything we do.

There is one critical area that often gets overlooked on a very personal level in families and close relationships. The courage to ask for help is often times what separates a willing helper from a person in genuine need of help.

As we build and strengthen our character, it is the courage to ask for help that can create massive momentum in strengthening our close relationships and having a positive impact to overcome some area of struggle in our lives.

We could spend a great deal of time discussing why we don't ask for help, but suffice to say, many of us do not reach out for help when we truly need it. We typically march on until disaster strikes and our cover-up has lost its effectiveness.

It may not be what we see on the news or read on the internet, but I am a firm believer that in most of our homes, schools, neighborhoods, and workplaces, people are genuinely willing to help someone in need. What we all lack is someone with the courage to ask.

Yes, we all can, and need to, improve our listening skills and our ability to discern the real question behind the question or the real comment behind the comment. However, **experience would tell us that we are all very good at the "cover-up."** We are very effective at continuing to attend the costume party and wearing our best mask.

As a parent, we would give anything to hear about the real struggles of our children to offer help and assistance in overcoming a challenge. Many times, children (of all ages) don't ask.

As a spouse, we would benefit much more from hearing what is at the heart of the struggles that often times manifest themselves in other ways like defensiveness, stonewalling, or contempt that cover up the real need for help. Many times, spouses don't ask, or they give up after a few years of asking.

As a friend, we would open the door to much richer relationships if we went beyond the "everything is fine, things are great" comment and genuinely opened up and asked for help. Many times, friends don't ask.

There are a number of benefits that can come about when we have the courage to ask for help:

- We bring clarity to the need. Our relationships often wander with unproductive energy spent trying to figure out what is at the heart of the struggle or a particular behavior.

- We provide someone who wants to help with the opportunity to productively help. There is often times a willing helper without the understanding of where or how to help.

- We demonstrate to others the necessary courage to be vulnerable and ask for help. Our example will help them build courage to ask for help during their time of need…and we all have times of need.

Many times, the complexity of our lives will hinder our ability to know exactly how to describe what it is we need help with—we just know the reality that we are hurting. A simple, soft call for "help" can open the door for a more productive discussion than simply maintaining the cover-up until disaster strikes and the costume party ends.

As we demonstrate the courage to ask for help, we will build and strengthen our character, and *Character Creates Opportunity* to build stronger relationships with those closest to us.

Questions to Dig Deeper

When in my life was I afraid to ask for help?

What small step can I take to be more courageous and ask for help?

Weekly Reflections

What have I learned and/or how have I grown in the prior week?

_____

_____

What are my hopes for the week ahead?

_____

_____

What three things am I thankful for that could be a source of encouragement to me in the week ahead?

(1) _____

(2) _____

(3) _____

How am I serving and sacrificing in the important areas of my life?

Family and Friends: _____

_____

Work: _____

_____

Community: _____

_____

What small steps can I take this week to continue to build and strengthen my character?

In my thoughts:

_____

In my decisions:

_____

In my actions:

_____

37

JUST KEEP MOVING FORWARD

"Experience is the mother of all learning," so the saying goes. We all have some defining experiences in our lives.

If we look back, there are probably a few events in our school years that we can still recall having a major impact on our lives. Whether it was a big championship game, an interaction with a great teacher, or some unfortunate painful experience, we still carry those experiences throughout our adult years. There are definitely some experiences from our close relationships, probably some positive and some negative, which remain with us as we continue our journey. Likewise, there are experiences in our chosen career that became teachable moments for us and we have carried those lessons with us to this day.

During my time in the Army, I certainly had some experiences that stay with me to this day. I learned a great deal about myself and a great deal about leadership, courage, strategy, and tactics. When I reflect back on the most significant learning, it was quite simple; the importance of just keeping moving forward. Whether tired, scared, or confused, just keep moving forward toward your objective. As an infantryman, with a heavy pack, leading a platoon of soldiers, the pressing call was always to keep moving forward toward the objective. Whether it was to complete a long, difficult road march, a specific tactical scenario that needed to be mastered in total darkness, or whether it was securing an objective on the battlefield in Iraq. No matter the ups and downs in that pursuit, there was a clear calling to just keep moving forward no matter what came our way.

Applying the principle to keep moving forward to our general journey of life would remind us that we know what the objectives are in serving a cause greater than our own, building a strong family, and a purposeful career. We know there will be unavoidable difficulties and very painful experiences that we will encounter. There will definitely be things we said or did that we genuinely wish we could take back and "do over." However, there are no "do overs" in the life we are living. There is a need to be intentional about what we learn from those experiences, and we just need to keep moving forward in the direction of our objective.

It is important that we accept the reality that "do overs" don't happen in this life. Many times, the damage is done, and perhaps only time can bring about some healing. We cannot "re-raise" our children, "re-live" some difficult moments in relationships, or "re-live" that career choice of 10 years ago. First impressions cannot be remade. Mean-spirited comments cannot be restated. Scars, many times, cannot be completely removed.

Life can only be lived in the present moment. What we have today is a great opportunity to keep moving forward regardless of the pain from the past. We will build and strengthen our character as we continue to move forward towards our objective, and our *Character Creates Opportunity* to build healthy relationships and puts us on the most effective path to accomplish our hopes and dreams.

Questions to Dig Deeper

In what area of my life have I hesitated in moving forward?

What small step can I take to keep moving forward in an important area of my life?

Weekly Reflections

What have I learned and/or how have I grown in the prior week?

_____

_____

What are my hopes for the week ahead?

_____

_____

What three things am I thankful for that could be a source of encouragement to me in the week ahead?

(1) _____

(2) _____

(3) _____

How am I serving and sacrificing in the important areas of my life?

Family and Friends: _____

_____

Work: _____

_____

Community: _____

_____

What small steps can I take this week to continue to build and strengthen my character?

In my thoughts:

_____

In my decisions:

_____

In my actions:

38

STAY

As we continue on our journey of building and strengthening our character, an important point to remember is that there is no finish line.

When I speak in seminars on the topic of the journey of life, I often reference three realities along our journey: (1) There is no finish line with regards to our impact on the relationships around us. Even in death, the legacy of our relationships lives on in the lives of those left behind. (2) All important relationships endure some significant ups and downs. (3) When we choose to guide our thoughts, decisions, and actions by principles like honesty, compassion, and sacrifice, we strengthen our character and our relationships. When we fail to guide our thoughts, decisions, and actions by those same principles, we weaken our character and our relationships.

It is not uncommon in these discussions that the topic of personal sustainability comes up. How can we sustain our efforts along this journey when we are told (a) there is no finish line (in essence, what is our pace for a race that has no finish line?), (b) there are some significant high points combined with some pretty significant low points, and (c) we need to take responsibility for the relationship even though it "takes two to tango."

Below are three suggestions that I often offer to provide some support and encouragement to keep moving forward and I hope they are uplifting to you as well.

Stay Humble: We really do reap what we sow as defined in the Law of the Harvest. This is a very well-worn, principled path to achievement. Although life is not always fair, more times than not, if we set a goal, make a plan to achieve that goal, work hard over time on delivering on the plan, we will reap a harvest and accomplish the goal. We need to be careful not to let the momentum of our success build our pride as we will have a tendency to miss warning signs of pending challenges and our decision-making will start to rely on our own track record and fail to take the counsel of others. If we do not stay humble, the transparency that is our new reality has a tendency to crush our pride in very public and painful ways. Stay humble.

Stay Hungry: One of the biggest threats to building and strengthening our character and our relationships is when we get complacent and comfortable. When we deny the reality that our journey will be filled with ups and downs, we get comfortable and complacent in so-called "good times." We fail to spend energy learning and growing in our relationships. When our bellies are full, the bills are paid, and the sun is shining, we still need to hunger after raising the bar on ourselves and our relationships by delivering on the basics: serving more than taking, understanding more than judging, and listening more than talking. Stay hungry.

Stay in the Ring: No one is perfect and we all fall short from time to time. It is important that we do not quit the fight when we make mistakes. We should stay in the ring and keep fighting the good fight. There is no more important game in town than building and strengthening our character and our relationships to have a positive impact along our journey. Don't choose to become a spectator, no matter how many times we fall short. Stay in the ring.

As we stay humble, stay hungry, and stay in the ring, we will build and strengthen our character, and *Character Creates Opportunity* to strengthen our relationships and have a greater impact in our homes, our businesses, and our communities.

Questions to Dig Deeper

What was a recent low point in a close relationship when I felt like walking away?

What small step can I take to stay in the ring and work on a close relationship that is struggling?

Weekly Reflections

What have I learned and/or how have I grown in the prior week?

_____

What are my hopes for the week ahead?

_____

_____

What three things am I thankful for that could be a source of encouragement to me in the week ahead?

(1) _____

(2) _____

(3) _____

How am I serving and sacrificing in the important areas of my life?

Family and Friends: _____

_____

Work: _____

_____

Community: _____

_____

What small steps can I take this week to continue to build and strengthen my character?

In my thoughts:

_____

In my decisions:

In my actions:

39

ON THE EDGE OF DESPAIR

Let's face it. There are times in our lives when we face the toughest of circumstances and we stand on the edge of losing hope.

Whether it is a close relationship that has unraveled and the reality of "happily ever after" seems unreachable. Or maybe it is the teenage or adult child who has lost their way. Or maybe it is the hopes and dreams of a business that has just run out of cash and its demise is imminent. Or maybe it is the sense that the safety and comfort of the "good old days" are never coming back in our communities.

These are the times when all the money in the world could not buy a quick fix out of the situation and all the pump-up, positive thinking, motivation speeches sound like nails on a chalk board.

As we continue on our journey to build and strengthen our character, it is on the edge of despair where we can find opportunity to learn and grow through difficulty.

On the edge of despair is where our masks come off and the costume party we have been attending comes to a close. In the very raw, unguarded, and openness of pain, when we have no strength to hold up the mask of "everything is fine," we now can begin to move forward on the path to learning and growth.

On the edge of despair, there are several things to consider as we look to build and strengthen our character through these moments of opportunity:

- The most effective direction to move is forward towards the hurt and embrace the unguarded, authentic moment of pain. Take the mask off to begin to grow.

- Be intentional about avoiding the routine addictions we have learned to cover the pain. We all have our own ways of coping to keep the costume party going. Growth comes when we realize the party cannot go on forever.

- Communication in times of pain is real, genuine, and priceless for our growth. We should find someone we can trust and open up. If we do not have someone in our close circle to confide in, then we need to seek out a pastor or counselor as the pathway to health is accelerated with open communication of our pain.

- Our very best will emerge from the pain. Psychologists and our own experience would demonstrate that we only grow in struggles. "No pain, no gain" is not just a slogan for coaches during practice. We have a massive human weakness to get soft, complacent, and lazy during moments of calm and order. We should use the times of pain to grow…it is our only chance.

- No matter what the outcome of our present struggle, there is one positive step that can come out of any difficult situation. We can, and should, use our feelings of raw hurt to grow in empathy for others. Our pain can be a catalyst for our growth in compassion for the struggles of others. Another incredible accelerant on our pathway to health is when we turn to help others through their struggles.

When we stand on the edge of despair and we focus on growing through the struggle, we will continue to build and strengthen our character, and *Character Creates Opportunity* to remain on the path to our own emotional health and well positions us to be a helping hand to others.

One last point: When we turn the corner on this present struggle, we should remember that life will always have another interesting event waiting around the next corner. If we can address our present struggle in a healthy way, we will be in a better position to address the inevitable next bump in the road. Enjoy the journey!

Questions to Dig Deeper

When was I recently on the edge of despair?

What small step can I take to turn a difficult situation into a positive outcome?

Weekly Reflections

What have I learned and/or how have I grown in the prior week?

_____

_____

What are my hopes for the week ahead?

_____

_____

What three things am I thankful for that could be a source of encouragement to me in the week ahead?

(1) _____

(2) _____

(3) _____

How am I serving and sacrificing in the important areas of my life?

Family and Friends: _____

_____

Work: _____

_____

Community: _____

_____

What small steps can I take this week to continue to build and strengthen my character?

In my thoughts:

_____

In my decisions:

_____

In my actions:

_____

40

THE ROLE WE PLAY

Throughout history, our time and attention are drawn towards those who are out in front making the headlines, giving the speeches, and closing the big deal. Many times, those exalted as innovators, brilliant, effective leaders, or the ones making things happen, are often seen as being larger than life compared to the rest of us.

Most of us are not in the spotlight, on the stage, being interviewed by the reporter, or standing in the ribbon-cutting line.

As we continue on our journey to build and strengthen our character, this chapter is about the important role most of us play, the role of assisting others to reach their full potential.

The history books that document mankind's achievements or the scrapbook that documents the achievements made within our families may leave the "assistants" out of the biographies. However, the reality is that the lives of those who have public or private impact are most often filled with others assisting them in their efforts.

We all know well the inventions and legacy of Thomas Edison. However, we probably don't know William Hammer who was Edison's chief engineer responsible for most of the work at the Edison Lamp Company or Frank Sprague who was the mathematician behind critical steps in the electric lighting system. These assistants helped Edison reach his full potential.

We can probably name the head coach of our favorite football team, but I bet we struggle to name the offensive line coach who is often responsible for building the group of linemen who clear the path for the running back to get on the cover of a sports magazine.

Behind every well performing leader in business, there is always an assistant who makes sure things get done. Behind every sales position in an organization, there is usually a team of assistants making sure expectations are met. These assistants most often do not take the stage at the Million Dollar Round Table banquet, but without them, top performance is not possible.

Truth be told, our most underappreciated examples of honorable, quiet assistants occur with those closest to us in our homes and extended family. It is these assistants who form the backbone of health and safety in our communities and our nation. The service of one spouse to another, of a parent to a child, siblings to each other, and the service of children reversing roles to assist elderly parents makes all the difference in building a strong family.

If it weren't for the honorable and principled assistants, we would all be in a difficult position. The history books and our discussions at family gatherings may leave them out, but they are a critical element to purpose and accomplishment.

An important reality to accept, sooner rather than later, is that a passionate, purposeful life is not about personal achievement, rather it is about helping others reach their full potential.

Our efforts to faithfully play our role, which most likely will not make the headlines, will help to build and strengthen our character, and *Character Creates Opportunity* for us to assist others in helping them reach their full potential.

Questions to Dig Deeper

What people close to me assist me in reaching my full potential?

What small step can I take to demonstrate my gratefulness for their effort?

Weekly Reflections

What have I learned and/or how have I grown in the prior week?

_____

_____

What are my hopes for the week ahead?

_____

_____

What three things am I thankful for that could be a source of encouragement to me in the week ahead?

(1) _____

(2) _____

(3) _____

How am I serving and sacrificing in the important areas of my life?

Family and Friends: _____

_____

Work: _____

_____

Community: _____

_____

What small steps can I take this week to continue to build and strengthen my character?

In my thoughts:

_____

In my decisions:

In my actions:

41

A POWERFUL TOOL

There is a great deal of research and practical experience that demonstrates the power of the written word. Writing down thoughts and ideas has been proven to bring clarity to our thinking and improve our ability to understand, which enable us to more effectively change our behavior.

In today's world, there is plenty of advice from personal development gurus, life-coaches, kitchen table psychologists, etc. who would tell us that goals not written down or plans that are only talked about rarely materialize into an accomplishment. Written words enable us time to reflect, think more clearly, and in turn, take action more effectively.

As we continue on our journey to build and strengthen our character, the written word becomes a powerful tool to make meaningful progress towards any endeavor. "Winging it" is not a sustainable proposition in today's world that continues to grow in complexity. Written goals and plans help form the foundation for steady progress.

The below are a few areas of practical application to leverage the power of the written word:

1. **A personal journal.** Throughout history, there have been numerous examples of people of impact who developed the habit of keeping a journal to help shape their attitudes, reinforce their direction in the

important areas of life, and continue to make progress towards reaching their full potential. There are a number of techniques, tools, and resources available to help us, but at the end of the day, we need to choose one that works for us and develop the habit. We will be following in the footsteps of some pretty effective people and we should be confident that we will make progress in our ability to have a positive impact.

2. **Written letters to others.** With today's abundance of online chatter, it should not be lost on anyone that we rarely are givers or receivers of a genuine, well-thought-out letter of appreciation, thanks, or encouragement. With the exception of the nice birthday card, holiday greeting, or a line or two of abbreviated text via social media, we probably have not received or given a well-thought-out letter in a long time. Some researchers have found that receiving a written word of encouragement is more effective than any other form of communication.

In my own journey, I have found two helpful reminders that put a little fire under me to raise the bar in reaching out to others with a thoughtful and meaningful written letter:

1. When I look back over certain periods of my professional life, I have spent more time and effort writing to customers or comments to team members than I have in writing a note of encouragement or appreciation to other people in the more lasting areas of my life…perhaps you have too.

2. Observing the example of others who are raising the bar. A number of years ago, a close friend shared a story with me that has stayed with me and consistently reminds me of how important the written word can be to strengthen relationships. When he and his siblings went away to college, his father wrote them a letter every single day for four years. It was not a short letter. Each letter was a handwritten, single-spaced, two-sided piece of paper describing how proud he was of them, that "the family" was behind them, and how he continued to encourage them to reach their potential. My friend described many of the wonderful things their father did for them and their family over the years, but that single act of letter writing throughout their college years, which demonstrated such dedication, commitment, and encouragement, had the greatest impact during their formative years.

That story continues to be a good reminder to me and hopefully to you, that we should raise the bar on our efforts and effectiveness with the written word to the people who matter most in our lives. I can almost guarantee they will appreciate it.

As we build some habits around the importance of the written word, we will build and strengthen our character, and *Character Creates Opportunity* for us to be more effective in the essential areas of life.

Questions to Dig Deeper

When was the last time I wrote a note of encouragement to someone I care deeply about?

What small step can I take to use the written word to help reach my full potential?

Weekly Reflections

What have I learned and/or how have I grown in the prior week?

_____

_____

What are my hopes for the week ahead?

_____

_____

What three things am I thankful for that could be a source of encouragement to me in the week ahead?

(1) _____

(2) _____

(3) _____

How am I serving and sacrificing in the important areas of my life?

Family and Friends: _____

_____

Work: _____

_____

Community: _____

_____

What small steps can I take this week to continue to build and strengthen my character?

In my thoughts:

_____

In my decisions:

_____

In my actions:

_____

42

THE UNSPOKEN REQUEST

Over the last 15+ years, our collective sense of security has continued to erode in our communities and the world. The tragedies that we have witnessed continue to get more shocking as we all journey through uncharted waters, and we find it difficult to make some sense of our new reality.

This chapter's topic is not going to solve the world's security challenge, but it will focus on something closer to home. As we work to positively impact those closest to us, the hope is that the ripple effect of that collective impact can help to counteract the trends of our day. There is an unspoken request within each one of us, that when acted upon, can strengthen the foundation of our well-being and best position us to reach our full potential.

When you look back into the history of your life, did you ever have someone who believed in you even when everyone else seemed to bail on you, including yourself? Someone who stayed with you regardless of the situation? Did you ever have someone who did not give in to you while also not giving up on you? If so, who is that person? Just for a moment, can you recall those experiences that impacted you so deeply?

For each one of us, there is an unspoken request for a person like that in our lives. Academic psychologists and our own life experience would say that having a person in our life who believes in us, through the good times and most importantly the bad times, is a critical element to our own well-being and will help enable us to raise the bar on our own potential.

As we continue on our journey to build and strengthen our character, the challenge for each one of us is not to search for someone like that, but to strive to be "that person" to those we care about most. We build and strengthen our character in the service of others when we meet this unspoken request in those around us.

As we look to meet that unspoken request in others and be "that person" who keeps the hope of potential alive in good times and in bad, here are a few simple and practical ideas to help:

1. Listen…really listen for the content being described and the emotion being felt. Listen with the intent to stand in their shoes and know what it feels like. Without getting too scientific, the most practical way for us to start is to just shut up for a moment. Our chatter does not help us understand. We already know what we think. Turn our attention toward others.

2. Be thoughtful and resolute in the consistent reinforcement of timeless and universal principles…there is still truth and relevance to principles like honesty, commitment, loyalty, and duty. These principles are a helpful way to remind others about an effective path forward when behavior has gone astray without letting "our opinion" be an obstacle to shining light along the path of a very dark journey.

3. Provide a clear, unmistakable sense that "I am with you." Those closest to us need to feel it and see that we are not going to bail when the going gets tough…and it will get tough. We are not perfect and in tough situations our imperfections often get magnified, but we should always come back to reinforcing the point that "I am with you."

Our challenge today is to resist the temptation to wish for and search for "that person" for ourselves, but instead proactively be "that person" for those close to us. The practical reality we all know to be true is that what comes around, goes around, and we will attract others who learn to share in our mutual effort to meet the most important unspoken request within all of us.

As we make the decision to be "that person" who believes in someone, even when they do not believe in themselves, we will build and strengthen our character, and our *Character Creates Opportunity* for us to have a lasting positive impact on others and reach our full potential in our journey of life.

Questions to Dig Deeper

Who in my life could I be "that person" for and reinforce that I believe in them?

What small step can I take to show that I believe in them?

<u>Weekly Reflections</u>

What have I learned and/or how have I grown in the prior week?

_____

_____

What are my hopes for the week ahead?

_____

_____

What three things am I thankful for that could be a source of encouragement to me in the week ahead?

(1) _____

(2) _____

(3) _____

How am I serving and sacrificing in the important areas of my life?

Family and Friends: _____

_____

Work: _____

_____

Community: _____

_____

What small steps can I take this week to continue to build and strengthen my character?

In my thoughts:

_____

In my decisions:

_____

In my actions:

_____

43

AN EFFECTIVE COMBINATION

As we continue on our journey to build and strengthen our character, there is the occasional need to remind and reinforce the truth that there are no quick and easy solutions to address the major challenges in life or to accomplish our major goals in life. As the saying goes, "If it were easy, everybody would be doing it."

Despite the reality that there are no easy fixes, we continue to be baited and many times hooked to the idea of "3 simple steps" to awesome relationships, the "10-minute workout" that will keep us healthy and fit, or by simply answering the "one big question" we will energize our team to win in the marketplace.

When I hear those "simple and easy" pitches, I am reminded of the quote by Michelangelo, "If people knew how hard I worked to get my mastery, it wouldn't seem so wonderful after all."

There are a number of techniques that can help us increase our personal effectiveness, achieve some goal, or support our team to reach a key milestone. These techniques may change with the times and the technology, but there are two principles that will help to determine our level of effectiveness over the long haul.

The first principle is **Education**: Formal education in high school, college, or graduate school will certainly play a part. However, for most adults, continual, ongoing education throughout life is the critical factor. When we remain open to learn from others, from our experiences, from mentors and friends, take a new class, read a book, or watch an educational video on the internet, we continue to grow. When we make a choice to remain closed to continually educating ourselves, we fail to grow. Failing to grow is a problem no "quick fix" will overcome.

The second principle is **Effort**: There is no substitute for the energy required to work hard and persevere. The significant achievements in life don't come about from quick wit, smooth talking, or the one brilliant solution; they come about from good old fashion effort over time, just like we learned as kids. Building and maintaining healthy relationships, especially those in the home, takes an enormous amount of intentional effort. The "happily ever after" stories we read as kids fell short on that reality. However, our life experience reinforces the reality that intentional effort over time is the foundation for healthy relationships.

In addition to being a good reminder for all us, I especially wanted to highlight these principles for two specific groups of people:

1. For those who are currently in a tough struggle to reach a goal and anxiousness, worry, and doubt are draining precious energy. My hope is that this will be an encouraging reminder of the truth that education and effort are the foundation of achievement. Reaching a goal is not about being the smartest, having the best connections, or just plain luck. Education and effort will play to our favor in the long haul, so keep moving forward on those two fronts no matter how tough the present struggle.

2. For those who still may be holding out hope that there is that secret, quick-fix formula out there to reach our hopes and dreams. My hope is that this chapter could be a sobering reminder to you and those you influence that the secret, quick-fix to the important things in life is not a reality. Education and effort will always play a part in the foundation for achievement.

As we continue to increase our effort and our ongoing education, we will build and strengthen our character, and *Character Creates Opportunity* to improve relationships, overcome challenges, and reach our goals.

Questions to Dig Deeper

When was the last time I was tempted by a "quick and easy" solution to a challenge?

What small step can I take to act on the principles of effort and education to reach my goals?

<u>Weekly Reflections</u>

What have I learned and/or how have I grown in the prior week?

_____

_____

What are my hopes for the week ahead?

_____

_____

What three things am I thankful for that could be a source of encouragement to me in the week ahead?

(1) _____

(2) _____

(3) _____

How am I serving and sacrificing in the important areas of my life?

Family and Friends: _____

_____

Work: _____

_____

Community: _____

_____

What small steps can I take this week to continue to build and strengthen my character?

In my thoughts:

_____

In my decisions:

_____

In my actions:

_____

44

THE IMPACT OF INFLUENCE

As we continue on our journey to build and strengthen our character, one foundational principle is the importance of accepting responsibility for our own thoughts, decisions, and actions as a core component to character building. Accepting responsibility is the first step in rising above our situation and escaping the trap of blaming others or our surroundings for the choices we make.

Accepting personal responsibility is important. It does not mean we always make great choices. The reality is that we will fall short in some of the decisions we make and actions we take. No one is perfect and we all make mistakes. Our character is strengthened when we fully accept the effective and the ineffective choices we make and the positive and negative outcomes that they may bring about.

An important dimension to accepting responsibility is acknowledging our influence on others. Yes, each one of us owns our decisions, but we all play a role of influence on others:

- Students make the decision to learn in the classroom, but a great teacher can raise the level of engagement and interest to make the classroom a more conducive environment to learn.

- A great coach can inspire teamwork and commitment, but ultimately it is the decision of individual players to work together as a team.

- A strong leader in the workplace can build energy, excitement, and efficient systems to keep the team heading in the right direction to accomplish goals, but it is the day to day decisions of individual team members that sustains top performance in the marketplace.

- The examples we all set in the home have influence on those closest to us.

What happens when those in our circle of influence stumble and fall through poor choices and bring about a difficult outcome? One truth we should not back away from is that they must own it and make more effective choices moving forward to get back on track and head in a better direction.

However, there is an important element that often gets overlooked in the heat of the moment as we are sorting through the damage of a poor decision by someone close to us; The role we played around influence. An important question we need to ask ourselves is, "What could I have done differently?" We all have the ability to influence others. Could the decisions I made and actions I took have influenced a more effective choice that would have yielded a better outcome?

"What could I have done differently?"

A genuine self-assessment around this important question and a commitment to improve will help each one of us be more effective in our ability to positively influence others and help others make more effective decisions.

In terms of moving forward after someone close to us stumbles, there is one additional step that can influence a better tomorrow. Extend a helping hand to get back on track as opposed to leaving someone alone in the struggle. This is especially important in the home. Extending a helping hand, again, and again, and again, and again to those closest to us will help to build and strengthen our home and set an example of understanding and compassion that is missing many times in sustained family conflict.

As we acknowledge our role as influencers and guide our thoughts, decisions, and actions by principles like encouragement, loyalty, and commitment, we will continue to build and strengthen our character, and *Character Creates Opportunity* to influence others in a positive way and help those around us reach their full potential.

Questions to Dig Deeper

When was the last time I asked myself, "What could I have done differently?" in dealing with someone I care about?

What small step can I take to be a more positive influence on those I care about most?

Weekly Reflections

What have I learned and/or how have I grown in the prior week?

_____

_____

What are my hopes for the week ahead?

_____

_____

What three things am I thankful for that could be a source of encouragement to me in the week ahead?

(1) _____

(2) _____

(3) _____

How am I serving and sacrificing in the important areas of my life?

Family and Friends: _____

_____

Work: _____

_____

Community: _____

What small steps can I take this week to continue to build and strengthen my character?

In my thoughts:

In my decisions:

In my actions:

45

THE COST

We all have a few areas in our lives where we wish things were "a little better."

Perhaps it is the sales of a certain product line at work, a tough relationship with a disappointed customer, the grade in a difficult subject in school, the strained relationship in our home, or the social trends in our community. Toss in our own personal financial situation or our growing waistline and I am sure we can all find an area or two where we wish things were "a little better."

Reaching a sense of fulfillment and emotional health in knowing that we actually made progress in doing "a little better" is going to take some effort. More often than not, the effort required usually involves a change in behavior. We are all probably familiar with Albert Einstein's definition of insanity: "Doing the same thing over and over again and expecting different results." Nothing happens without change.

As we continue on our journey to build and strengthen our character, the question we need to address is, "What is it going to take to get 'a little better' in that important area of our life?"

Many times, we know, or someone tells us, what that small incremental change in behavior needs to be. In places like work and school, there is usually a consistent roadmap to follow and we just need to make the choice, step-up the effort, and deliver. There is a cost of time and effort, but it is pretty predictable and the choice to follow the roadmap is ours to make.

The more difficult decisions are in the areas that really matter in the long haul of life, like our close relationships and the legacy of our efforts and accomplishments. In these important areas, there may not be a clear roadmap and the near-term costs may seem quite high:

- To mend a strained relationship, many times we need a desire to be reconciled rather than to be proven right, we need to shut up and seek to understand as opposed to giving our opinion, and/or we need to extend favor when the natural tendency would be to fight back.

- To impact our legacy, many times we need to sacrifice in the near term to ensure a brighter tomorrow. Whether that is saving today versus spending to have some money for the rainy day that will come, grinding it out in a job so that those closest to our care can have opportunities we did not, or taking a risk and following a different path than we were "supposed to follow."

As we all consider the costs in these big and important areas of life, we need to be reminded that there is a relatively small cost of trying and failing when compared to the significant cost of regret that comes with not trying at all.

We will build and strengthen our character as we keep "trying," and our **Character Creates Opportunity** to do "a little better" in the big and small areas of life. Based on my experience and the experience of so many around me, I want to extend a word of encouragement to those who continue to try: Keep getting after it, it is worth the cost.

Questions to Dig Deeper

In what areas of my life do I feel I could "do a little better."

What small step can I take to "do a little better?"

Weekly Reflections

What have I learned and/or how have I grown in the prior week?

_____

_____

What are my hopes for the week ahead?

_____

_____

What three things am I thankful for that could be a source of encouragement to me in the week ahead?

(1) _____

(2) _____

(3) _____

How am I serving and sacrificing in the important areas of my life?

Family and Friends: _____

_____

Work: _____

_____

Community: _____

_____

What small steps can I take this week to continue to build and strengthen my character?

In my thoughts:

_____

In my decisions:

_____

In my actions:

_____

46

PREVENTION

We have all heard of the guidance provided by Ben Franklin with the saying, "An ounce of prevention is worth a pound of cure."

The clarity and truth brought forth in that simple statement can be applied to various areas of our lives such as our health, relationships, work, and community.

As we look to continue to build and strengthen our character, an important area to consider is not only that we understand the concept of prevention, but that we have some very practical steps to take to ensure we are dedicating a significant amount of effort on the side of prevention.

The relatively easy approach to prevention can most certainly be found in regard to our health: Eat a well-balanced diet, get regular exercise, sleep 7 to 8 hours a day, schedule annual wellness check-ups with a physician, and proceed with the rule of thumb around moderation in all areas. The basic tenets of maintaining physical health have been relatively unchanged over the years. Consistently executing on a preventative health program is another story, but the basic plan is straight-forward.

The more challenging area of prevention is taking the practical steps necessary to maintain health in our most important relationships.

Life, despite its complexity, is still predominately about relationship to others. Whether those relationships are with family, friends, community, or the workplace, we are in relationship with others.

What does an "ounce of prevention" look like in maintaining health in relationship?

Here are just a few suggestions:

Keep Commitments. Actually doing what we say we are going to do, is a simple, but massive step forward in maintaining health in relationships. "I will be there on time," "I will clean up this mess," "I will support you no matter what." When we fall short too many times on our promises, we will need more than a pound of cure to re-establish health again.

Focus on Serving. Serving the needs of others on a consistent basis has been shown throughout recorded history as being one of the most critical elements to maintaining health in relationships. Our personal intent to serve others rather than waiting to be served will keep us on the most effective path toward healthy relationships.

Sacrifice. Nothing worthwhile ever comes easy. Sacrificing our selfish instincts in favor of supporting others, demonstrates to others that we recognize life is not all about us. Setting a personal example of sacrifice is contagious and helps to form a strong foundation of health in relationships.

Physical Connection — Touch. There has been a significant amount of research done on the positive impact that a simple physical touch can have on maintaining health in a relationship. The physical connection made with the touch on a shoulder, the holding of a hand, or a genuine hug builds health into relationships.

Life is continuing to grow in complexity and intensity. In order to be able to sustain our efforts for the long haul, using "ounces of prevention" instead of "pounds of cure" will help us stretch our limited resources to ensure we have optimal impact.

As we make choices to focus daily effort on prevention to maintain health, we will build and strengthen our character, and *Character Creates Opportunity* to sustain optimal physical health, to build healthy relationships, and to head down a path to build a legacy with few, if any, regrets.

Questions to Dig Deeper

What relationships have I neglected to give an "ounce of prevention" to keep healthy?

What small step can I take to support health in my closest relationships?"

Weekly Reflections

What have I learned and/or how have I grown in the prior week?

_____

_____

What are my hopes for the week ahead?

_____

_____

What three things am I thankful for that could be a source of encouragement to me in the week ahead?

(1) _____

(2) _____

(3) _____

How am I serving and sacrificing in the important areas of my life?

Family and Friends: _____

_____

Work: _____

_____

Community: _____

_____

What small steps can I take this week to continue to build and strengthen my character?

In my thoughts:

_____

In my decisions:

_____

In my actions:

_____

47

WHAT DO YOU SEE?

There is no doubt that we live in a complicated world that seems to steadily grow in complexity and intensity.

As we continue on our journey to build and strengthen our character in order to reach our full potential, there are points in time when we just need a simple reminder of truth to help us carry on. When there seems to be a never-ending cycle of uncertainty around the globe, in our communities, and in our homes, we all could benefit from a reminder of universal, timeless, and self-evident truth to help us keep moving forward in a world that can sometimes leave us dazed and confused.

A simple reminder of truth today is that we become what we think about…we become what we "see" in our mind's eye. Whether we subscribe to the teachings of some famous personal development guru, some "enlightened" individual, or we believe in the Book of Proverbs that says, "As a man thinks in his heart, so is he" our take-away is the same. Regardless of our reference point, the truth remains, we become what we "see" in our mind's eye.

We don't need a PhD in psychology from a prestigious university, to be a member of the 1% or the 99% in terms of financial wealth, or to sit in a corner office to understand the simple, timeless, and universal truth that we become what we see in our mind's eye. We could reference numerous academic studies, cite quotes from individuals who have had real impact in our world, or think back along our own experience, and the conclusion would be the same…what I dwell on in my mind, so much so that it becomes crystal clear, I become.

As we build and strengthen our character, an important question we need to ask ourselves is, "What do I 'see' today?" In our own mind's eye, not in the view of a spouse, a parent, a boss, a teacher, a TV broadcaster, a mentor, but what do we "see" in our own view?

Do we see adversity that we cannot overcome? Do we see relationships that are best to be broken instead of repaired and strengthened?

Or…

Do we see an opportunity to rise above? Do we see challenge and a view of overcoming? Do we see the reality of close relationships struggling in the near term, but in the long view, see love, forgiveness, and togetherness?

Do we see a business with present-day challenges, but opportunity on the horizon? Do we see communities divided, but a pathway to cooperation and support?

Or…Do we just see dark clouds all around us?

Each one of us has the freedom to choose what we see in our own mind's eye.

What do you "see" today?

In this present time of challenge in our world and in our homes, it would be helpful to remember the simple truth that we become what we see in our mind's eye and ensure our lens is adjusted to see our present challenges as an opportunity to overcome and reach our full potential as individuals, families, and communities across the globe.

As we remind ourselves to refocus our mind's eye with principles, like patience, perseverance, hope, and faith, we build and strengthen our character, and *Character Creates Opportunity* for us to create the future we desire and rise up to reach our full potential.

Questions to Dig Deeper

In what situations do I normally see the negative and not the positive?

What small step can I take to see the opportunity and not the obstacle?

Weekly Reflections

What have I learned and/or how have I grown in the prior week?

_____

_____

What are my hopes for the week ahead?

_____

_____

What three things am I thankful for that could be a source of encouragement to me in the week ahead?

(1) _____

(2) _____

(3) _____

How am I serving and sacrificing in the important areas of my life?

Family and Friends: _____

_____

Work: _____

_____

Community: _____

_____

What small steps can I take this week to continue to build and strengthen my character?

In my thoughts:

_____

In my decisions:

_____

In my actions:

_____

48

THE AVOIDANCE STRATEGY

Psychologists, social researchers in academia, and our own personal experience would say that the vast majority of us avoid having the difficult conversation to address lingering frustrations that inevitably come with relationships in the home, the workplace, and the community.

Leaders in the workplace often delay having the difficult performance discussion with an employee until it is just unavoidable, and the team or project has been significantly impacted.

Couples in the home often avoid the known stress points or triggers in the relationship and keep their fingers crossed that it will just go away without a fight this time.

Communities often look the other way and sweep problems under the rug until one small action ignites a firestorm of the now unavoidable reality.

As we continue on our journey to build and strengthen our character, demonstrating the wisdom and courage to address the difficult and uncomfortable topics will help us prevent the cancer of delay from spreading and destroying the long-term health of close relationships.

Emotion is often bound to a moment, but wisdom is always married to time.

We need wisdom to be effective in dealing with the complexity of life and that only comes with time and experience.

Here are just a few thoughts to address the avoidance strategy head on:

1. **Acknowledge the Truth.** It is not easy to effectively have these types of discussions. Life is often sloppy and painful, and addressing difficult issues does not come with paint-by-numbers instructions. It is not perfect, but it needs to be experienced, not avoided.

2. **Begin the Dialogue.** When we avoid addressing the problem, we often create more problems. Unresolved issues do not go away, they just rear themselves in other ways. We learn and grow as we address challenges, so get started.

3. **Intent and Understanding are the Foundation.** It is important to be genuine in our intent to move the relationship forward in a healthy way to achieve the long-term goals of the team, the family, or the community. Seek understanding first as we do not see the world as it is, but we see the world as we are, and our experiences and attitudes bring about a host of preconceived notions and biases.

4. **Don't Lose Hope.** We may often find ourselves in a tough spot in our homes, our close relationships, and in our community. We will learn and grow through addressing difficult issues and even if they don't get adequately resolved, we will be setting a great example for those closest to us that we don't give up. Keep hope alive.

As we strive to reach our full potential in our lives and in our relationships, we will always have difficult issues to address and the avoidance strategy is just not an effective option. We learn and grow as we work through difficult issues and the wisdom we gain will help us build and strengthen our character, and *Character Creates Opportunity* to reach our hopes and dreams.

Questions to Dig Deeper

What difficult conversations do I avoid having on a consistent basis?

What small step can I take to stop avoiding a difficult conversation?

<u>Weekly Reflections</u>

What have I learned and/or how have I grown in the prior week?

_____

_____

What are my hopes for the week ahead?

_____

_____

What three things am I thankful for that could be a source of encouragement to me in the week ahead?

(1) _____

(2) _____

(3) _____

How am I serving and sacrificing in the important areas of my life?

Family and Friends: _____

_____

Work: _____

_____

Community: _____

_____

What small steps can I take this week to continue to build and strengthen my character?

In my thoughts:

In my decisions:

In my actions:

49

A FEW STEPS TOWARD REDEMPTION

Let's face the truth. All of us have made mistakes, fallen short of goals, and had a few really painful disappointments in life.

There has been a great deal written about a recent trend by many academics to build résumé of their failures to demonstrate to students (and the world) that we all have failed numerous times in the pursuit of goals in order to better prepare students for the real world.

Given that we have all fallen short, the opportunity for redemption, or helping us to become more acceptable, especially in the eyes of those closest to us, is extremely relevant as we continue on our journey to build and strengthen our character and reach our full potential. The opportunity for redemption is very appealing to meet a most important human need beyond the basics, the need to know we matter and are accepted by those around us.

Like most efforts in reaching our full potential, the steps towards redemption are no different, we have some internal work to do on ourselves and we have some external effort we can offer those around us.

Internal Steps:

The inward journey towards redemption begins with a good inventory of those times we have fallen short. The easy part is the concrete shortfalls in a career journey, academics, financial failures, etc. The really hard part, but most meaningful inventory, includes the times we have fallen short in the relationships closest to us; a lost temper, a hurtful word, or a rejection when we were needed most. That is the list that hurts the most.

This type of inventory helps in two important ways (1) The list keeps us grounded and humble. The Scriptures warn us that "pride comes before the fall," so we all should want to avoid that painful reality as much as possible. (2) The list helps us to be less judgmental of those around us. We have a tendency to not be as critical when we have some self-awareness of our own shortcomings.

External Steps:

The external journey towards redemption begins with a word of encouragement to others. Offering an encouraging word to others is many times the gateway for developing a deeper relationship with someone close to us. We live in a world that emphasizes the negative and an encouraging word can be like oxygen to someone suffocating in an environment of negativity and pessimism. We all carry a few heavy burdens known only to ourselves and an encouraging word is a helpful boost as we journey along.

Encouragement, especially to those closest to us, can help in a few important ways (1) Helps others feel better about themselves and begin to feel they matter (2) Creates an environment where others may become more open to share struggles without the fear of judgment and shame (3) Enables others to move forward in their own journey even if it is silently alone.

These internal and external steps are necessary on the continual journey towards redemption. The journey towards redemption is ongoing in the real world as life is not stagnant. We encounter new people, new experiences, new challenges, and ultimately a few more of our own failures along the way. Similar to the phrase "life is a journey not a destination" so can be said of the process towards redemption with those closest to us in our homes and families.

As we continue to move forward with these steps towards redemption, we will build and strengthen our character, and ***Character Creates Opportunity*** to build strong and healthy relationships with those that matter most.

Questions to Dig Deeper

In what area of my life do I need to be redeemed?

What small step can I take to move closer towards redemption with the people I care about most?

<u>Weekly Reflections</u>

What have I learned and/or how have I grown in the prior week?

_____

_____

What are my hopes for the week ahead?

_____

_____

What three things am I thankful for that could be a source of encouragement to me in the week ahead?

(1) _____

(2) _____

(3) _____

How am I serving and sacrificing in the important areas of my life?

Family and Friends: _____

_____

Work: _____

_____

Community: _____

_____

What small steps can I take this week to continue to build and strengthen my character?

In my thoughts:

_____

In my decisions:

_____

In my actions:

_____

50

ARE WE THERE YET?

Are we there yet? We are all very familiar with the question that comes at some point during a long drive. Depending on how long the drive or how much stress has been injected into the preparations for the drive, there will be a wide array of follow-on responses to that simple question.

So often we attribute that question to a young child on a road trip. However, many of us as adults may find ourselves asking a similar question on our journey of life.

When will we be happily married? When will our children be able to stand on their own?

When will I be in a stable and fruitful career? When will we finally have peace in our home and community?

When will I finally be done with getting an education?

As we continue on our journey to build and strengthen our character, how we cope with the adult version of the question "Are we there yet?" will help us grow our joy and peace as we journey along to reach our full potential.

We all celebrate the accomplishment of significant milestones. The awarding of a graduation diploma, the winning of a championship, the anniversary of a relationship milestone like 25 years of marriage, 30 years of dedicated employment, and the list could go on. At the time of crossing the threshold of accomplishment, there is joy, celebration, and some peaceful relief in knowing we finally made it.

As time inevitably marches quickly through the threshold of any specific accomplishment, many times we forget the graduation speech, we misplace the thoughtful anniversary card, and we forget the leftover cake in the company lunchroom.

The reality about what remains with us after the accomplishment and brief celebration pass, is not the celebration, it is the memories and lessons learned along the journey that remain.

- We remember the courage and strength it took to study all night for numerous exams to ensure we passed that tough course. Those memories act as a rallying cry to strengthen our character to ensure we can rise above again when we are faced with another challenge down the road.

- We remember the pain and the joy of years spent in a close relationship like marriage and those reminders help give us perspective when the next jolt to the foundation of a close relationship comes in the future...and it will come in the future. It is that perspective which will help to carry us through the inevitable dark time in our committed relationships.

- We remember the business lessons learned from good and bad decisions we made in the marketplace. It is the memory of these lessons that gives us confidence to re-enter the marketplace and attempt to grow a business again.

Setting clear goals to be accomplished is a critical part of reaching our full potential. However, we need to ensure we maintain the perspective that goals are simply milestones to gauge our progress on the long journey. We will inevitably pass through those goals and will need to continue to set further milestones down the road.

The energy needed to reach our full potential in a long and fruitful life does not simply come from accomplishing goals. The renewable energy for life is in leveraging the memories and lessons learned along the journey. This renewable energy will ensure we consistently raise the bar on our ability to positively impact those around us.

As we continue to maintain our perspective when answering the adult version of "Are we there yet?" and we focus on learning along our journey, we will build and strengthen our character, and our *Character Creates Opportunity* to accomplish the next big goal or milestone.

Questions to Dig Deeper

In what area of my life do I continue to ask, "Are we there yet?"

What small step can I take to find peace in the journey?

Weekly Reflections

What have I learned and/or how have I grown in the prior week?

_____

_____

What are my hopes for the week ahead?

_____

_____

What three things am I thankful for that could be a source of encouragement to me in the week ahead?

(1) _____

(2) _____

(3) _____

How am I serving and sacrificing in the important areas of my life?

Family and Friends: _____

_____

Work: _____

Community: _____

What small steps can I take this week to continue to build and strengthen my character?

In my thoughts:

In my decisions:

In my actions:

51

DON'T COUNT ON IT

We often wish for a quick fix to move rapidly through some challenging times.

- Financial struggles — We wish the lottery numbers would come our way or that long lost Uncle Harry shows up on the doorstep with a briefcase full of money...don't count on it.

- Business struggles — We wish our first product would be the "must have" product for the market and we struggle to keep up with demand...don't count on it.

- Family struggles — For the most painful of all of life's struggles, those in the home, we wish those dark times in a marriage or those "know it all" teenage attitudes could just be avoided...don't count on it.

- And why can't our YouTube video go viral like so many others? Don't count on it.

Although it may seem like a great option, the quick fix to struggles actually does more harm than good. There is an overwhelming amount of evidence that shows a quick fix is not the most effective path to reach our full potential. When a quick fix arrives, we end up numbing our senses and most often unhappy when the "fix" fades away; and the "fix" always fades away sooner than we think it can.

As we continue on our journey to build and strengthen our character, it is important that we make the choice to embrace the struggle of the journey as we would not want it any other way. It is highly unlikely that the lottery solves our problems, the next big thing scales our business, and somehow we enter a period of family bliss like the TV shows of our youth.

Below are a few reasons to help encourage all of us to embrace the struggles and enjoy the fact that we will need to work hard for a long time to succeed in the marketplace, save our marriage, and raise our children effectively in this uncertain and complicated world.

1. **A sense of peace from a "hard day's work."** There is no quick fix that can surpass the peace experienced after successfully enduring a long struggle. Whether that is the completion of a difficult physical workout, the reflections after a graduation, the silver or gold anniversary celebration, or the signing of a major business transaction. We rise above the pain of the struggles and reflect peacefully on the journey that we walked through to reach a major goal. No quick fix can match that feeling of overcoming through a long journey.

2. **Continual learning and personal growth.** The reality is that we only learn through the struggles. Ask any coach at any level of play. Teams learn more from a loss than a win. We learn more from poor product launches than when they go well. Struggles bring personal growth and growth leads us down the path to reach our full potential.

3. **Setting the example for others to follow.** Whether it is coworkers, family members, or friends in the community, we are being observed. We set a strong example for others to follow when we embrace the opportunity of the struggle. The spirit to continue is contagious and we light a spark for someone else to continue in their own, often unspoken, difficult struggle.

As we face the reality that a quick fix to our problems is not in the cards and we learn to embrace the struggles of hard work, disappointment, and outright confusion, we will continue to build and strengthen our character, and *Character Creates Opportunity* to reach our full potential.

Questions to Dig Deeper

In what area of my life am I still hoping for a quick fix?

What small step can I take to embrace the hard work and the ups and downs needed to make a difference in my life?

Weekly Reflections

What have I learned and/or how have I grown in the prior week?

_____

_____

What are my hopes for the week ahead?

_____

_____

What three things am I thankful for that could be a source of encouragement to me in the week ahead?

(1) _____

(2) _____

(3) _____

How am I serving and sacrificing in the important areas of my life?

Family and Friends: _____

_____

Work: _____

_____

Community: _____

_____

What small steps can I take this week to continue to build and strengthen my character?

In my thoughts:

In my decisions:

In my actions:

52

THE MOST IMPORTANT BASE OF OPERATIONS

When I was a young infantry officer with the 101st Airborne Division, we always started a mission from a base of operations. When we were on a small patrol, we would establish a patrol base to secure and then send small teams out for various missions. On a much grander scale, we established and occupied Forward Operating Base Cobra, 90 kilometers inside Iraq during the First Gulf War. As a young leader, it was very effective to have a home base. The home base was secure (for the most part), it was where key updates on the enemy situation were provided, a new mission was disseminated, and weapons and food were replenished.

Recent events across the globe and in our own country, consistently remind us of the challenging times we live in today. As we continue on our journey to build and strengthen our character, it is important for us to maintain a base of operations to effectively deal with uncertainty and change.

During challenging times, we have a tendency to look to large groups or organizations for the "great ideas" or the foundation to deal with the challenges we face today. Political leaders and leaders in education, business, churches, and community groups play an important part in supporting our ability, as individuals and as a society, to effectively deal with change and challenge. However, the base of operations with the greatest potential to deal with change and challenge is the family.

The foundation of the family has the potential to be the most effective base of operations for support in dealing with a challenging world. Family is where many first learn:

1. The value of education from a parent reading to a young child

2. The value of sacrifice by seeing a parent work in and/or outside the home to provide

3. The value of service by seeing a family member serve our nation, our community, or others in need

4. The value of compassion by seeing family gather around a sick loved one

5. The value of living an intentional life as we remember the legacy of grandparents and parents

Most teachers would agree that the critical factor in the growth and development of a student is not some new curriculum or assessment tool, it is family involvement. When families care about the education of their children, they learn and grow at a much greater rate.

The same can be said about so many other aspects of society. It is the foundation of family that helps minimize crime, poverty, and many of the ills of society. It is the foundation of family that also ignites that first spark of innovation, dreams, and passion that set a course for positive change in our world.

For all of us, it does not matter what kind of home base of operations we came from or what condition our family is in today. We cannot rewrite the past.

What matters most is what we do going forward to build a strong base of operations to help our family deal with change and challenge.

We will always remain a son or daughter, a brother or sister, a parent or grandparent, a spouse or ex-spouse. The foundation of family will always be with us.

As we build and strengthen our character, an important question we need to continually ask ourselves is, "What are we doing to establish an effective base of operations within our family?"

Here are a few ideas:

1. **Be Intentional.** If we "wing it," we will fall short of our potential. The risks are too great. We need to be intentional about our thoughts, decisions, and actions within the home.

2. **Find Time.** Time is a great asset to the family. For many families, evenings provide an opportunity for greater connection or greater disconnection. We need to be careful in this day of personal electronics that we all don't "go to our separate corners" and miss an important chance to connect in the evenings.

3. **Create Conversation.** Just talking is a great start for many of us. Taking it to the next level would be having a conversation to truly understand the concerns of the day and be a listening ear to a voice that needs to be heard. We need to create a forum for conversation and be prepared to listen.

4. **Build Hope.** Our world is full of challenges and not enough encouragement. The base of operations for a family should be the source of hope for a better tomorrow and a bright light on the path to reach our dreams. The family should be that one point we can all count on to ensure hope is alive as we continue our journey.

As we guide our thoughts, decisions, and actions based on principles, like understanding, patience, and perseverance, we will build and strengthen our character, and *Character Creates Opportunity* for our family to be a strong base of operations for us to deal with change and challenge in our lives.

Questions to Dig Deeper

In what area of my home life do I still see consistent struggles?

What small step can I take to support and strengthen my family?

Weekly Reflections

What have I learned and/or how have I grown in the prior week?

_____

_____

What are my hopes for the week ahead?

_____

_____

What three things am I thankful for that could be a source of encouragement to me in the week ahead?

(1) _____

(2) _____

(3) _____

How am I serving and sacrificing in the important areas of my life?

Family and Friends: _____

_____

Work: _____

_____

Community: _____

_____

What small steps can I take this week to continue to build and strengthen my character?

In my thoughts:

_____

In my decisions:

_____

In my actions:

_____

LAGNIAPPE

*(From the Cajun-French term, lagniappe, meaning
a little something extra given at no cost)*

This chapter is "a little something extra" as a tribute to my Dad and Mom, Anthony and Mabel Esposito, who continue to build a legacy that inspires me to reach my hopes and dreams.

What Two Immigrants Taught Me

Immigration has always played a significant role in the history of the United States. In recent years, the debate has intensified with mostly extreme views on both sides taking up most of the air in the room. Given the ongoing and important dialogue around immigration, I wanted to utilize the forum of the Character Creates Opportunity blog to provide a personal moment of reflection on a principle that was taught to me by two immigrants I know very well.

The timeless, universal, and self-evident principle I learned from two immigrants was that *SERVICE* to a cause greater than my own is the gateway to making a positive impact and reaching one's full potential. In addition, I have seen this principle embodied in the efforts of countless numbers of immigrants I have come to know throughout my 50 years on this planet.

The two immigrants who taught me the principle of service to a cause greater than my own are my mom and dad. My mother came to this country by herself at the age of 18 from Glasgow, Scotland. My father is a second-generation Italian immigrant.

Family

As my mother came to this nation by herself, it was the open door of her sister who came to America a few years earlier that provided her with an initial foothold to get started. It was not a perfect support structure, but it enabled her to get her start on building a new life.

My father's family made their way initially in a shared apartment with close relatives. They got their start in the fresh produce business starting off with a wagon on a street corner and eventually moved to a modest storefront offering customers access to quality produce to a growing post-WWII population.

Families made sacrifices to ensure their loved ones had a helpful hand to initially find their way. The importance of service to family above oneself has been a recurrent theme throughout the lives of my parents. When the stresses and strains of raising a family, maintaining a marriage, and dealing with financial pressures would typically lead to the break-up of a family, my parents modeled a commitment to a greater cause than themselves and kept our family together.

Work

As my mom worked and journeyed along to make her new life, she met my father in their common place of work at a local bank in Hackensack, NJ.

Work, not as a means to build wealth, but as a means to serve others and provide the resources for a warm home to grow a family has been another recurrent theme throughout the lives of my parents. Whether sweeping floors or working in the corner office, work was viewed as a source of strength and self-worth when the barriers of different languages and cultures can sometimes drive feelings of insecurity and shame.

Community

As our family grew together there was always an element of service to our community that helped ensure we collectively lived safely and provided an opportunity for others to achieve their hopes and dreams.

The importance of service to a community and a nation has been a recurrent theme throughout the lives of my parents. Whether it was seeking elected office on our town's council, teaching in a community college, volunteering in local charities, and supporting youth athletics and education, my parents made it a priority to serve the community in which we lived to make it a better place for others to build a better life.

The priorities of family, work, and community based on the principle of service to a cause greater than oneself is what two immigrants taught me.

As I reflect on what I have witnessed in my own life, I have seen the principle of service to a cause greater than oneself displayed in the immigrants who were soldiers in my command in combat during the First Gulf War. In my 25 years in the healthcare marketplace, I see immigrants displaying the same willingness to serve a cause greater than themselves as they help to build businesses, ensure a solid home-life and community for their families, and pursue noble advances in science and technology.

There are several important by-products of the principle of service to a cause greater than ourselves that immigrants have taught me:

1. Service to a cause greater than ourselves keeps us humble despite how much outward success we may achieve in the world.

2. Service to a cause greater than ourselves provides an inner-peace that is a strong barrier to feelings of depression, negativity, and contempt for life. Science now proves that aspirations like focusing on helping others rewires our brains to more positive pathways that enable us to feel better, live healthier, and have a more positive impact on others.

3. Service to a cause greater than ourselves fills our hearts and minds with compassion for others and helps us be more empathic to the struggles of others. We become more compelled to help rather than judge, shame, or hurt.

Yes, it is true that there is no simple answer to the complexity of immigration in this modern era. There are people who want to come to this country to do harm and we need to provide for the necessary protection of our citizens. We do not have unlimited resources to fully address every need, so tough choices need to be made. We need a principle-based, respectful, and honest debate to come to the most effective solution.

However, the foundation of this nation has been built on the principle of **SERVICE** to a cause greater than oneself and that principle is the dominant theme that drives most immigrants to our nation. Unfortunately, that truth is many times lost by all of us who have never known or never taken the time to reflect on the origins of our own family tree that arrived in this land of opportunity.

What two immigrants taught me is that when service to a cause greater than oneself becomes our foundation, we become our best selves and make a positive impact on our world. As we focus on the principle of **SERVICE** we build and strengthen our character, and ***Character Creates Opportunity*** to make this world a better place.

Questions to Dig Deeper

What legacy do I want to leave for the people I care about most?

What small step can I take to start to build that legacy today?

Resources from Harvest Time Partners

Reality: We all struggle to have difficult conversations around the important things in life with those we care about most.

Face to Face
A unique set of resources to support families, educators, and counselors in opening a door to more effective communication about real-world, difficult issues and encouraging face-to-face discussion to improve decision-making and relationships. Available for various ages

Abundant Harvest for Kids and **Abundant Harvest for Teens & Adults**
A patented, award-winning board game to support effective communication, reinforce principle-based decision making and the Law of the Harvest; simply, you reap what you sow.

The Principles of Our World Children's Book Series
It is never too early in the development of a child to start talking about the importance of principles like compassion, honesty, courage and teamwork. The Principles of Our World books provide parents and teachers with the opportunity to teach children how **The Principles** can help them in a variety of situations they will experience in life.

For more information and to order these resources go to
www.harvesttimepartners.com

ABOUT THE AUTHOR

David is a combat veteran, business executive, husband, father, and creator of character-building resources that help individuals and families reach their full potential in an uncertain world.

After launching his business career as a sales representative, David quickly rose through the ranks of corporate America, advancing to the position of President and Chief Executive Officer of several innovative medical diagnostics companies that have made significant contributions in the areas of allergic disease and the early detection of cancer.

David's character and leadership skills were cultivated at West Point and through leadership assignments in the US Army Infantry. As a young infantry officer, David led a rifle platoon of 38 men with the 101st Airborne Division through several combat operations in the Gulf War. He was recognized with a Bronze Star for combat operations in February 1991.

David and his wife Tracy develop programs and resources designed to strengthen the character of individuals and build and sustain healthy relationships. This includes Character Creates Opportunity®, an initiative that was specifically designed to improve the character development of children, adolescents, and adults. Their patented, award-winning conversation game, Abundant Harvest®, is played by families, schools, counseling programs, and faith-based organizations worldwide as it opens a door to more productive dialogue and encourages decision making based on principles such as honesty, loyalty, and commitment. Reinforcing the Law of the Harvest, the game's primary lesson is the age-old adage that you will always reap what you sow. They also have created a conversation card game called Face to Face® that helps to foster effective conversations on real-world issues and to develop the critical life skill of face-to-face communication in a world that is rapidly changing how people connect.

David holds an MBA from Syracuse University and a bachelor's degree in civil engineering from West Point. He has appeared on CBS, NPR, and PBS and has been featured by many other news outlets.

David is available to provide support to individuals, families, and organizations on a variety of topics, encompassing building a strong marriage and family, personal and executive development, and leadership training.